Singing in the Spirit

A Devotional Collection
for Music Ministry

Mary Kay Beall

Code NO. 8007
ISBN 0-916642-65-8

© 1998 Hope Publishing Company
380 South Main Place, Carol Stream, IL 60188

This collection is gratefully dedicated to my first mentor
Audrey Mieir
whose talents and leadership and faith
left an indelible imprint on my life
and to
Trinity Lutheran Seminary
in Columbus, Ohio
where my talents and faith
were challenged and nutured and strengthened.

Table of Contents

Devotions by Theme Categories

ADVENT/CHRISTMAS
An Advent Promise
God of the Unexpected
Joy to the World!
Prepare the Way!
What Happens in the Silence?
Who Would Send a Baby?
Worrying Our Way to Christmas

ALL SAINTS' DAY
Those Weary Saints

BAPTISM
Take Me to the Water

CARE FOR CREATION
Is This My Father's World?

DISCIPLESHIP
Come, Follow Me
The Great Commission
A New Perspective on
Servanthood
Put Your Whole Self In

GENERAL SPIRITUALITY
ISSUES
Annual Check-Up
Bedeviled?
Bless the Lord, O My Soul!
Coming in First
Did Anybody Bring the Map?
Entering into God's Presence
Erasers Are the Nicest Things
Faithfulness or Faith Fullness?
Forgiveness . . . For What?
Getting Away From It All
I Don't Have Time to Pray!
I've Got a Secret!
The Last Word
Make a List!
Meditation on a Mystery

Plenty to Eat and Going Hungry!
Praise Is a State of Mind
The Shape of Things to Come
Telling Stories
Temper! Temper!
Through Thick and Thin
Welcome to the Middle Ages!
What's That in Your Hand?
When in Doubt, Look Up!

LIVING IN COMMUNITY
An Answer to Violence
Feeling Like the Lone Ranger?
Life in the City
Living in Common Time
Welcoming the Stranger

LENT/EASTER
Because He Cried
Lent Is Not My Favorite
Time of Year!
Life in Three Dimensions
A Nasty Surprise
What's Love Got to Do with It?
You Are There!

MUSIC
The Choir as Family
Dreaming Big
Doing a New Thing!
Music: A Fair and Glorious Gift
Paying Tribute
Professing Our Faith in Song
A Psalm for the Choir
Sing a New Song!
Whole Notes, Etc.

PENTECOST/HOLY SPIRIT
God Present in Us
Take a Deep Breath

THANKSGIVING
ThanksLiving

PREFACE

Most churches have a choir. It may be a very small group or it may be a large group . . . 50 or more. It may be a group of limited ability or it may be a group of skilled singers. The director may be a volunteer or a salaried member of the church staff. He or she may be professionally trained or merely a music lover with some degree of talent and leadership ability. Wherever your choir falls in the spectrum, one thing is certain. The choir members are, for the most part, volunteers who love to sing and who give their talents to their church as a gift. They are usually members of the church and in that capacity have some level of spiritual interest and commitment; it is my experience that, on an ongoing basis, the members of a choir generally give more time to the church, year in and year out, than any other member of the congregation.

I have been working with choirs professionally for nearly forty years. I took my first position at age sixteen as Cherub Choir Director in an Episcopal Church. Since then I have experienced all kinds of choirs and worked in a variety of denominational settings. Over the last ten years I have become increasingly aware that although many choir singers may have rich individual spiritual lives, most choirs have little or no corporate spiritual life. Why is this? For one thing the ongoing agenda is a demanding one and many directors are pressed to cover the things in rehearsal that absolutely must be prepared for upcoming services. In addition, many directors see Spiritual Formation, i.e. prayers, devotions, etc. as something they *might* do on occasion, time permitting, but not as a necessary part of the rehearsal agenda. And, many directors might support Spiritual Formation activities but do not feel comfortable leading them.

In 1992 I began leading retreats for choirs to help them begin to develop their personal spiritual lives and ultimately to work toward corporate spiritual life together. I do not think of the choir as a *performance* group. The choir is a group of singers who *minister* through music to the people, and who assist the congregation in offering *their* song to God in worship. This does not imply that sloppy musicianship is acceptable. After all, we should offer our *best* gifts to God in worship and that means that we render the music to the best of our ability. But technical perfection is not always synonymous with ministry and undue concentration on perfection can, in fact, cause a choir to lose its perspective on *why* they are singing in the first place.

A spiritually grounded choir can be a source of power that can enrich worship and the church as a whole. The choir can become a family within the larger family of faith, encouraging and upholding and praying for one another. They can pray not only for themselves and for their own music ministry but for the leaders of the church, for the pastors and for the members of the faith community. A committed, praying, spiritually strong choir will sing differently and there will be a dimension to their music that will reach further and deeper than before. The singers will be empowered and enriched by their membership in the choir and that empowerment will spill over into the congregation.

You may be saying, "Well, that sounds *wonderful*, but I would never know how to begin." And I would answer, begin with a brief devotional time in your rehearsal, a time that is faithfully set aside, a time that is *not* negotiable. Include that allotment of time in your rehearsal planning. Let the choir know that you are committed to this and why . . . that you believe that it will uplift them and enhance their music ministry and their personal lives as well. If your choir has no experience with devotions in the rehearsal setting, don't be heavy-handed. Don't hit them with too much too fast. Whatever you do, do not allow the devotional time to be open-ended so that the rehearsals run over or the music does not receive adequate rehearsal. Choir rehearsal is *not* a prayer meeting! It is a rehearsal. The director and the singers are charged with the responsibility of preparing the music to the best of their ability for the enhancement of worship. But, by the same token, the choir is not primarily a social club. Social activities should be a part of their experience together but there must be something happening in the rehearsal that defines the choir as *believers* who sing.

This book, *Singing in the Spirit*, is designed to provide devotional materials that are spiritually provocative, timely, and brief. Each devotion includes a scripture, a hymn reference which usually may be read *or* sung, a meditation and a brief prayer. Each devotion includes three questions for reflection. In most cases, one question relates specifically to the hymn, one is general and one is directed to musical concerns. If you choose to do the "bare bones" devotional, you may omit the questions altogether or you may encourage a brief discussion of one of the questions. If time permits, you may choose to use them all.

I have collected and read a wide variety of devotional materials in preparation for writing this book. After due consideration, I determined that a "measured" format for the meditation and the prayer would give the material a more poetic reading and would provide a more unique look to each page. Compare an excerpt first in a prose format and then in a "measured" format and judge for yourself:

It's hard to get caught up in heavenly mission when our hardened hearts and our muddled minds are focused on earthly things.

It's hard to get caught up in a heavenly mission
when our hardened hearts
and our muddled minds
are focused on earthly things.

I included a hymn reference with each devotion because I feel strongly that hymns should be a part of our ongoing life as believers. The hymnal is an invaluable devotional tool as well as a collection of faith statements of believers spanning several centuries and continents. There is depth of thought and experience in hymn texts that deserves to be preserved and employed and valued as a part of our ongoing devotional experience. Louis Fitz-Gerald Benson (1855–1930) one of America's leading hymnologists wrote: "Hymns that are not made personally familiar by devotional reading have not much spiritual influence. It is only the precedent appropriation of the hymn's message by each individual heart that makes its congregational singing worthwhile."

With these things in mind, I strongly encourage you to include a hymn text as part of your devotional time together, even if you only use a single stanza. I attempted to select hymns and choruses that appear in most hymnals and that cross denominational lines. However, if the hymn reference is unfamiliar or unavailable to you or if you have another hymn that you feel would address the theme equally well, I urge you to use it.

If you as director are uncomfortable leading devotions with the choir, consider selecting a choir Chaplain or Chaplaincy Committee (call it what you will) to take this responsibility. Make certain the designated leader(s) understand the time constraints and abide by them for the sake of the musical demands of the rehearsal.

Unless you are new to a position, you are likely to have some idea of where your choir stands in terms of spiritual life. In a spiritually-centered, lively church, it would be surprising to encounter a choir that was not of like mind. Some choirs have already established a basic devotional routine which, at the very least, includes a prayer time at the close of rehearsal. You will need to evaluate where your choir stands on this issue before you begin so that you do not overwhelm them with too much or underestimate them with too little.

As my retreat ministry grows, I have become aware that choirs are at all stages in the area of spiritual interest and commitment. Some choirs are spiritually motivated because the Pastor of the church promotes a strong spiritual life for the whole church. Some are motivated because the Music Director is a deeply spiritual individual. And some choirs independently form a spiritual oasis in the midst of a troubled faith community.

Some directors have scheduled a Friday evening or a Saturday time for me to come and introduce their choir to the spiritual possibilities that are available. Some choirs who have regular annual retreats have asked me to spend the weekend with them and to plan a series of varied events that will focus on spiritual formation. While the director often sets the overall agenda for a choir, some choirs have approached their leader requesting a weekly devotional time in the context of rehearsal. And, some choirs have invited my husband, John Carter and myself to come together for a weekend with a dual agenda: Choral Training and Spiritual Formation.

I have included some materials in the back of this book which I hope will be of help to you in leading your choir into a more intentional spiritual life. You will find a list of "Practical Ideas for Choir Singers Who Want a Richer Spiritual Life", a Bibliography of materials that you can purchase or recommend to your choir, and my personal version of the Ten Commandments adapted for Church Choirs which will give you an interesting slant on your ministry in the church.

Please note the following:

1. Scripture references are from the NRSV edition of the Bible unless otherwise noted. If you prefer another translation you need to have it handy.

2. The choir will need to have hymnals available for the devotional time. Make sure the hymn for that evening is in your hymnal.

3. In cases where the hymn reference is not a standard hymn, I have included the music in the Appendix. You may copy the hymn for devotional use but you must secure permission for any use in a worship setting.

4. If you should wish to print any of the meditations or prayers for use in a worship service you should obtain permission from the publisher.

Martin Luther said:

Music is a fair and glorious gift of God.
I would not for the world forego my humble share of music.

I am strongly persuaded that after theology
there is no art that can be placed on a level with music;
for besides theology
music is the only art capable of affording peace and joy of the heart.
The devil flees before the sound of music
almost as much as before the word of God.

There is something unique about Music and about its power to convey the gospel message. Those of us with special musical talents and gifts bear a responsibility before God to use those God-given gifts for the good of the Kingdom and to lead those in our charge in their understanding of *their* own responsibilities as gifted believers ministering to others through music. It is my hope and my prayer that the material in this book will encourage you and your choir in your faith journey and will enrich your musical experiences as well. If you would like to share any particulars of your choir's spiritual growth, I would be happy to hear from you. And if you would like further information about planning a retreat together, please contact me through Hope Publishing Company (1-800-323-1049) or at my home:

Mary Kay Beall
Singing in the Spirit
31 East Gates Street
Columbus, Ohio 43206
Phone (614)444-5610
Fax (614)444-5680

An Advent Promise

Scripture Reading: Isaiah 40:4

Every valley shall be lifted up and every mountain and hill be made low; the uneven ground shall become level and the rough places a plain.

Hymn Reference:

O Come, O Come, Emmanuel Latin hymn 12th c.
tr. John M. Neale, 1851; st. 5 Henry Sloane Coffin, 1916

Meditation:

I needed to hear those familiar words of Isaiah today.
Sometimes life can seem like a kind of wilderness . . .
one dark valley after another
one mountain after another
one uneven place after another
one rough spot after another.

I need to remember that He came
to make things better
to get us through the valleys
to get us over the mountains
to smooth the way
to even out the rough places in our lives.

I am thankful for His coming
for the promise that precedes it
and especially for the time of rejoicing
that is just up ahead.

Reflection:

1. Sing the hymn or read the text together. Some particular words or phrases might speak to your own situation just now. Do you feel "captive" to something in your life from which you would like to be set free? Do you feel surrounded by "shades of night" perhaps depressed or disillusioned? Are you troubled by feelings of "envy", "strife" or "quarrels" at work or at home? How can the refrain help you to cope with and overcome these "rough places" in your life?

2. If you are dealing with a particularly difficult issue would you be willing to share your difficulty with the group and ask for their prayers in helping you to cope?

3. As believers we are People of Promise. What promise means the most to you today?

Prayer:

O come, O come, Emmanuel!
Set us free from all the things that hold us captive.

O come, O come, Emmanuel!
Lift us up out of the dark valley into the sunshine.

O come, O come, Emmanuel!
Help us over the mountain we're facing.

O come, O come, Emmanuel!
Smooth out the rough places that are draining us of energy and joy.

O come, O come, Emmanuel!
Enable us to rejoice in Your presence and power.
Amen.

Annual Check-Up

Scripture Reading: Acts 2:42, 44–47

They devoted themselves to the apostles' teaching and fellowship, to the breaking of bread and the prayers. All who believed were together and had all things in common; they would sell their possessions and goods and distribute the proceeds to all, as any had need. Day by day, as they spent much time together in the temple, they broke bread at home and ate their food with glad and generous hearts, praising God and having the goodwill of all the people.

Hymn Reference:

A Charge to Keep I Have   Charles Wesley, 1762

Meditation:

It's getting time for the dreaded **Annual Check-up.**
I know I need to do it but I always drag my feet.
I worry about my blood pressure.
I worry about my weight.
I know I've gained a few pounds since last year.
I wish now I had kept up my health club membership
and my daily walk.
I know I'm going to hear about that.
And about eating healthier.
Oh, well, it's just once a year.

Thank God we don't have annual check-ups in church.
I'd have to admit to a lot of worrisome things I need to change
and frankly, I'd rather not confront them.
Maybe I **should** worry about my spiritual health.
I hardly ever pray anymore
and I can't remember when I last opened my Bible.
And I'm not as faithful in the Choir as I used to be
but frankly, I've been **so** busy lately,
Spiritual life takes time
and I don't seem to have any left over for non-essentials.
Nobody seems to notice though
and I'm not **really** accountable to anyone,
(pause)
Am I?

Reflection:

1. Sing the hymn or read the text together. According to the writer of the text, what responsibilities does the Christian have? To whom is the Christian accountable?

2. As a Christian do you feel you have a particular calling, a ministry? Do you consider singing in the choir a ministry? If you do, how does that affect the way you perceive your commitment and responsibility in the group?

3. If you were to give yourself a "Check-Up" on your spiritual life today, how would you rate yourself in these areas: Bible Study, Quiet Time, Church Attendance, Ministry and Mission, Evangelism?

Prayer:

O God of All Our Best Intentions,
forgive our indulgences
and our lapses,
forgive our excuses
and our justifications.
Encourage us to care for our bodies
to care for our minds
and to care for our souls
remembering that we ARE indeed accountable
to one another
and most of all
to YOU!
Amen.

An Answer to Violence

Scripture Reading: John 14:27

Peace I leave with you; my peace I give to you. I do not give to you as the world gives. Do not let your hearts be troubled, and do not let them be afraid.

Hymn Reference:

I've Got Peace Like a River Trad. Spiritual
See Appendix page 137

Meditation:

Pick up the paper or any magazine on the news stand.
What do you find on those pages every day?
Road rage!
Child abuse!
Drive by Shootings!
Abduction!
Rumors of War!
Divorces by the dozen!
Drug Raids!
Gang violence!
Robberies!
Murders!
Unwanted children!
New and more frightening military weapons!
Schools with policemen in the hallways!
Homes with frightened wives and children cowering in corners!

This is the world we Christians live in today.
This is the place where we are called to be salt and light.
This is the place where we are called to preach and sing the good news.

Remember that in the midst of all of this chaos
in the midst of all of this bloodshed and violence
in the midst of all of this pain and hunger and hardship
we have the gift of Christ's peace in our lives
to calm us when the world seems to much to bear
and to offer to those who need to know
that peace is available
in a violent and troubled world.

14

Reflection:

1. Sing the first stanza of the hymn together. Take hold of the gift of peace in your own life to meet the violence and hardship that churns around you.

2. Strive to maintain peace in your home, in your church and in your choir. What are some things you can do to this end?

3. Is there a particular hymn or anthem that expresses the sense of perfect peace for you?

Prayer:

Our hearts are hungry for peace, Lord.
Our nights and days are filled with violent words
and violent acts.
Calm us with Your perfect peace
and help us to offer that peace
to those whose lives we touch.
Amen.

Because He Cried

Scripture Reading: John 11:35

Jesus wept.

Hymn Reference:

O Sacred Head Now Wounded   att. Bernard of Clairvaux
tr. James Waddel Alexander 1804–1859

Meditation:

Jesus knows what it is to cry.

He cried over the death of a friend
a friend whose death he might have averted
a friend whom He had dearly loved.

He cried over Jerusalem . . .
yearning to save her from her own blindness
yearning to gather her to Himself
but she would not.

He cried in the garden . . .
frightened of what lay ahead
desperate for another way to the goal
betrayed by one of His own.

He cried on the cross
separated from His father
hurting in every fiber of His being
bearing the awful weight of the world's misdeeds.

Yes, Jesus knows . . . better than any of us . . .
what it is to cry.

Reflection:

1. Read the scripture accounts of the times when Jesus suffered and cried:

Jesus Weeps over the Death of a Friend	John 11:28–36
The Lament over Jerusalem	Lk 13:34–35
Jesus Prays on the Mount of Olives	Lk 22:39–46
The Death of Jesus	Mark 15:33–37

2. If God's own Son can suffer emotional pain, what does that say to you about the nature of God and God's response to our pain?

3. Read the text of the hymn together. What does the hymn-writer have to say about Jesus' suffering?

Prayer:

You know what it is to cry, Lord.
Well, today, we're the ones who are crying . . .
crying over relationships torn beyond mending
crying over lost opportunities
crying over things said and unsaid
deeds done and undone.

Today, Lord, we need to be comforted.

We come to You for that comfort.
Because You cried
we can lay all of our hurt
all of our pain
all of our anger
all of our frustration
all of our need
at Your feet.

We can survive every disappointment that life can bring
because You are present with us through it all
because You know what it is to cry.
Amen.

17

Bedevilled? Who Me?

Scripture Reading: Psalm 46:1–3, 7

God is our refuge and strength, a very present help in trouble. Therefore we will not fear, though the earth should change, though the mountains shake in the heart of the sea; though its waters roar and foam, though the mountains tremble with its tumult. The Lord of hosts is with us; the God of Jacob is our refuge.

Hymn Reference:

A Mighty Fortress Is Our God   Martin Luther
tr. Frederick H. Hedge

Meditation:

I don't like to think about devils.

I tell myself they are nonsense . . .
storybook stuff . . .
nasty, slimy creatures,
evil-eyed,
cloven-hooved,
slinking about in the darkness
doing whatever it is that devils do best.

No, I don't like to think about devils.
Why should I?
They have nothing to do with me.

I'm a Christian. They can't get me.
I don't have to peek under the bed at night.

I'm a Christian. They can't get me.
I don't have to whistle in the dark.

I'm a Christian. They can't get me.
Or can they?

Reflection:

1. Sing stanzas 1 and 3 of the hymns. What does Martin Luther have to say about the reality of evil and about God's power?

2. What do you see in today's world that illustrates the conflict of good and evil?

3. What "devils" do you have to contend with as a person of faith? As a choir member?

Prayer:

Lord, I don't like to think about devils
but something tells me this world is full of them.

Something tells me they are all around me . . .
tugging at my resolve
testing the waters of my commitment
nibbling at the corners of my good intentions
picking away at the delicate fabric of my faith.

Something tells me these real devils
Envy . . . Hate . . . Greed
Anger . . . Lust . . . Spite
Ego and Sloth
are threatening to undo me.

I don't like to think about devils, Lord,
but I must.

Something tells me I need a safe place
where they can't get at me.
Something tells me You are my safe place.
Amen.

Bless the Lord, O My Soul

Scripture Reading: Psalm 103:1–5

Bless the Lord, O my soul, and all that is within me, bless his holy name. Bless the Lord, O my soul, and do not forget all his benefits—who forgives all your iniquity, who heals all your diseases, who redeems your life from the Pit, who crowns you with steadfast love and mercy, who satisfies you with good as long as you live so that your youth is renewed like the eagle's.

Hymn Reference:
Bless His Holy Name   Andraé Crouch

Meditation:

The idea of blessing is an ancient one
and may have originated
in the sprinkling of blood
to consecrate or make holy.

It is a way of asking for divine favor
of expressing a wish for good fortune
or happiness
Blessing is desirable.
Who among us would turn down a blessing?

But blessing has another meaning.
It is a way of praising
a way of glorifying
a way of saying thank you.

So while we are anxious to **receive** God's blessing
on our own lives
we ourselves can **extend** blessing **to** God
in our praise
and in our thanksgiving.

We can say with the psalmist:
Bless the Lord, O my soul
and all that is within me
bless His holy name!

Reflection:

1. Can you finish this sentence in your own words, "Bless the Lord who . . ."?

2. Do you feel that your ministry in the choir is a way of "blessing" God? Can you explain why or why not?

3. Sing the hymn several times as a meditation. As you sing can you think of any "great things" the Lord has done in your life or in the life of someone you know?

Prayer:

(This prayer may be read as a litany with the choir repeating the first line together and the leader completing each thought)

May you be blessed forever, Lord,
for not abandoning me when I abandoned You.

May you be blessed forever, Lord,
for offering Your hand of love
in my darkest, most lonely moment.

May you be blessed forever, Lord,
for putting up with such a stubborn soul as mine.

May you be blessed forever, Lord,
for being constant and unchanging
amongst all the changes of the world.

May you be blessed forever, Lord,
for your countless blessings on me and on all your creation.

Amen.
(Adapted from Teresa of Avila, Spain 1502–1582)

The Choir Family

Scripture Reading: John 13:34–35

I give you a new commandment, that you love one another. Just as I have loved you, you should also love one another. By this everyone will know that You are my disciples, if you have love for one another.

Hymn Reference:

They'll Know We Are Christians by Our Love   Peter Scholtes

Meditation:

To be in a choir is to be part of a family,

a singing family
a Christian family
a committed family
a caring family
a praying family
a joyful family
a fun-loving family

To be in a choir is to minister to others through song.

To be in a choir is to be blessed.

Reflection:

1. Sing or read stanzas 1, 2 and 3 of the hymn together. What does the hymn say about the visible signs of a Christian community?

2. Is your choir a family? Do you share your joys and concerns with one another? Do you care for one another? Do you have fun together?

3. If you would like your choir to become more like a family, what things would you suggest to help them move in that direction?

Prayer:

Lord, behold our family here assembled.
We thank you for this place in which we meet
for the song that unites us
for the peace accorded us this day
for the hope with which we await tomorrow;
for the health, the work, the food and the bright skies
that make our lives delightful;
for our friends in all parts of the earth.
Give us courage and joy and a quiet mind.
Spare us to our friends, soften us to our enemies.
Bless us, if it may be, in all our endeavors;
if it may not, give us the strength
to endure that which is to come
that we may be brave in difficulty,
constant in tribulation, temperate in anger
and in all changes of fortune
down to the gates of death,
loyal and loving to one another.
As the clay to the potter
as the windmill to the wind
as children to their father
we ask your help and your mercy.
For Christ's sake.
Amen.
(Adapted from Robert Louis Stevenson by Mary Kay Beall)

Coming in First

Scripture Reading: Exodus 20:2b–5a

You shall have no other gods before me. You shall not make for yourself an idol whether in the form of anything that is in heaven above or that is on the earth beneath, or that is in the water under the earth. You shall not bow down to them or worship them for I the Lord your God am a jealous God . . .

Hymn Reference:

Sing Praise to God Who Reigns Above   Johann J. Schütz
tr. Frances Cox, 1864, alt.

Meditation:

I used to think that of all the commandments
the first was the easiest to keep.
"You shall have no other gods before me!"
That didn't seem too difficult.
I knew there was only one true God
but I hadn't yet experienced the temptations of real life.

What gods do **you** put before Him?
What comes first in **your** life?
Money?
Power?
Family?
Achievements?
Fitness?
Good works?
Pleasure?
An addiction?

Strangely enough
many of the things that take God's place in our lives
are **good** things in themselves
Desirable things
but not good enough to be **first** in our lives?
Not good enough to displace God!

Those of us who are Christians
and who serve God in the church
who hold places on committees
who prepare or serve communion
who sing in the choir
can actually get so involved in our service projects
our good works on behalf of God
that we put them **before** God.

What holds first place on your agenda?
Don't kid yourself!
Whatever that is
it is your God.

Reflection:

1. Sing the hymn or read the text together. Pay particular attention to the 4th stanza. What does the hymnwriter say about putting God in first place?

2. Make a list of the ten most important things in your life in order of importance. Go back and add the amount of time each week you spend on each item on the list. It may surprise you and cause you to revise the list.

3. With so much to accomplish in each choir rehearsal, it is easy to forget to pray. Is it possible to put God first in the choir and still get the job done? What changes could we make to establish a new priority?

Prayer:

O God
We sincerely desire most of all to give You first place in our lives.
Grant us the strength and determination to make that happen.
Amen.

Did Anybody Remember
to Bring the Map?

Scripture Reading: Psalm 107:30b

. . . and he brought them to their desired haven.

Hymn Reference:
Guide Me, O Thou Great Jehovah   William Williams

Meditation:

Taking a trip means
making a list . . .
all the things we mustn't forget
all the things we can't possibly do without
all the things we just **might** need.

Taking a trip means
planning for weeks, even months, in advance
leaving nothing to chance
remembering the travelers' checks
remembering to stop the mail
remembering to turn off the iron
remembering
remembering.

Finally it's time.
the bags are packed.
The car has a full tank of gas
and everything is loaded.
We are on the road at last
mentally ticking off our checklist
breathing a sigh of relief
putting aside our anxious fears.

Wait!
Where's the map?
Who has the map?
Someone **must** have it.
Does anybody know how to get where we're going?
For heaven's sake
how can we take a trip without a map?

Reflection:

1. Sing the hymn or read the text together. What lengthy trip does the hymnwriter recall in the text?

2. When did you last take a trip? Did you spend a lot of time preparing for it? Did You remember everything you intended to pack? Did you forget anything crucial?

3. What is the destination for this choir each week? Who has the map? Do we usually arrive safely and on time or do we end up forgetting something?

Prayer:

Lord, we wouldn't take a trip without a map.
We wouldn't attempt a rehearsal without a director.
How can we presume to travel through life
without Someone Who knows the way?

Pilgrims . . . that's what we are . . .
fumbling our way through new territory
surprises waiting at every turn
carrying more baggage than we'll ever need
and without a map
without a guide
without anyone to steer us
through the uncharted tangle of tomorrows.

Be our guide, Lord, on this uncharted course we call life.
We may be ill equipped for the trip
but, Praise God! **You have the map!**
Amen.

Doing a New Thing!

Scripture Reading: Isaiah 43:19a

I am about to do a new thing; now it springs forth, do you not perceive it?

Hymn Reference:

This Is a Day of New Beginnings Brian Wren

Meditation:

Christ calls us as believers to new life
to a new beginning.

"Old things are passed away.
Behold all things are become new!"

But this gift of grace, this new beginning,
has its roots in something centuries old
something traditional and well founded.

The church today is struggling to discover
what style of worship
what language
what music
will attract those who have fallen away from faith
or those who have never heard the good news at all.

Some churches are struggling to recover
from dissension
distrust
and disappointment.

Yes, we are called to something fresh and new
but we are also called to remember our tradition
to remember our roots
to hold on to the foundations of our faith
in liturgy
in worship
and in song.

We **are** called to a lively and fresh perspective on our faith.
We **are** called to new songs and new words and new ways.
But we are also called to cherish the roots of our tradition
to cherish the hymns
the prayers
the groundwork
that gave us our beginning

Reflection:

1. Sing or read the text of the hymn together. Does this hymn mention anything that is specific to your congregation?

2. Have you noticed any changes in your church's worship or liturgy or music? In your opinion, are these "new beginnings" effective or bothersome?

3. How do you feel about bridging the gap between tradition and new trends? What hymns or songs do you feel are the most successful at bridging the gap?

Prayer:

Lord of the old and Lord of the new
enliven this congregation and this choir
with a sense of adventure
and a willingness to explore
new ways
new words
and new forms of worship.

But as we make our way into the wilderness of the future
let us rely on the manna of the past to feed us on the journey.
Amen.

Dreams and Dreamers

Scripture Reading: Genesis 28:10–12

Jacob left Beersheba and went toward Haran. He came to a certain place and stayed there for the night, because the sun had set. Taking one of the stones of the place, he put it under his head and lay down in that place. And he dreamed there was a ladder set up on the earth, the top of it reaching to the heaven; and the angels of God were ascending and descending on it.

Hymn Reference:

We Are Climbing Jacob's Ladder   Trad. Spiritual

Meditation:

Are you a dreamer?
Scientists have proven that we all dream
but we don't all remember our dreams.
And when we **do** remember them
sometimes the content seems so foolish or impossible
that we dismiss the whole episode out of hand.

But dreams **can** be revelations.
Some cultures take dreams seriously.
What we dream can tell us things about ourselves
things we may not be aware of
things that we harbor far beneath the surface of our daily lives.
Dreams can provide a way for God to reach us
when our conscious defenses are down.

Jacob dreamed of a ladder reaching to heaven.
He was only one of many in the Bible
who dreamed strange dreams
that ultimately became crucial to their future.

Daydreams are a kind of dreaming that we do when we're awake.
Do you have dreams for yourself?
for your family?
for this church?
for this choir?

Don't be afraid to dream.
Dream big.
Pay attention to your dreams.
God may be trying to get your attention!

Reflection:

1. Sing the hymn or read the text together. Can you tell the story of Jacob's ladder and of what Jacob's dream meant?

2. Do you have a commonly recurring dream? Does it disturb you? Do you understand what it means? Is it urging you to move in some particular direction or is it reminding you of something you have repressed?

3. What do you dream for your church and your choir? Do you believe God can make it happen?

Prayer:

O God
you are the ultimate dreamer.
You dreamed the universe and made it a reality.
You dreamed all of creation and it became so.
You dreamed each of us and we were born.
You tell us we are made in Your image
so we must be dreamers too.
Help us, O God, to dream big dreams
for Your kingdom
for this church
and for this choir.
Amen.

Entering Into God's Presence

Scripture Reading: Psalm 42:1–2

As the deer longs for flowing streams, so my soul longs for you, God. My soul thirsts for God, for the living God. When shall I come and behold the face of God?

Hymn Reference:
The Lord Is in His Holy Temple   John Carter and Mary Kay Beall
See Appendix pages 138–139

Meditation:

Come now . . .
turn aside for a while from
your daily employment,
escape for a moment from
the tumult of your thoughts.

Put aside your weighty cares,
let your burdensome distractions wait,
free yourself a while for God
and rest a while in him.

Enter the inner chamber of your soul,
shut out everything except God
and that which can help you in seeking him,
and when you have shut the door, seek him.

Now, my whole heart, say to God,
`I seek your face,
Lord, it is your face I seek.'

(Anselm 1033–1109)

Reflection:

1. Sing the hymn together. Let the music set the tone for a time of silence before God.

2. Seek God's face in silence. Let silence be your prayer. Empty your mind and listen for God's voice.

3. Try to make silence a part of your private prayer time. Give God an opportunity to speak to you in the silence of your heart and mind.

Prayer:

Lord, teach me a new way to pray.

Teach me to pray without words.
Fill the silence, Lord, with Your presence.
Give me the patience to listen for Your voice.

Help me to find comfort
in silence.
Help me to find healing
in silence.
Help me to find You
in silence.

Amen.

Erasers are the Nicest Things

Scripture Reading: Psalm 103:1–3, 10–12 (NIV)

*Praise the Lord, O my soul; all my inmost being, praise his holy name.
Praise the Lord, O my soul and forget not all his benefits—who forgives all
your sins and heals all your diseases.*

*He does not treat us as our sins deserve or repay us according to our iniqui-
ties. For as high as the heavens are above the earth, so great is his love for
those who fear him; as far as the east is from the west, so far has he removed
our transgressions from us.*

Hymn Reference:
Amazing Grace   John Newton

Meditation:

Erasers are the nicest things.
What would we do without them?

When we make a mistake
as we are prone to do
an eraser is a handy thing to have around.
It can make a mistake go away
as if it never happened,
and we can start over
with a clean slate.

When we make a mistake,
as we are prone to do,
God's grace is a handy thing to have around.
It can make the mistake go away
as if it never happened,
and we can start over
with a clean slate.

Erasers are the nicest things!

Reflection:

1. Sing the first two stanzas of "Amazing Grace". How would you define grace? Why is God's grace "amazing"?

2. Why do you think this hymn is such a favorite with believers and unbelievers alike?

3. How does it feel to be forgiven? How does it feel to forgive?

Prayer:

O God
you have extended your unlimited grace to me
and made my life new.

You have erased the mistakes and misdeeds from my slate
and offered me a fresh start.
You have forgiven me
utterly and completely.

Enable me now to forgive myself.

Enable me now to forgive others
as I have been forgiven . . .
to extend Your amazing grace to them
as You have extended it to me.
Amen.

Faithfulness or Faith Fullness?

Scripture Reading: Luke 16:10; Galations 2:20a

Faithfulness: "Whoever is faithful in a very little is faithful also in much."
Faith Fullness: "And the life I now live in the flesh I live by faith in the
Son of God . . ."

Hymn Reference:

Blessed Assurance   Fanny J. Crosby

Meditation:

Are you faithful?
Do you keep your promises?
Do you shoulder your responsibilities?
Do you do your share?
Faithfulness means that **you** are worthy of trust
that others can rely on **you**!

Are you full of faith?
Faith**full**ness means that **God** is worthy of trust
that you can rely on **God**.

God wants **us** to be faithful
so that **others** can lean on **us**.

But God also wants **us** to be full of faith
so that **we** can lean on **Him**.

Reflection:

1. Read the hymn text aloud. The author, Fanny Crosby, says that this text is her story. It is her song. What is **your** story and **your** song?

2. Do you see yourself as a **faithful** choir member? Would others in the choir call you faithful?

3. What does your **faith** have to do with your membership in the choir?

Prayer:

Lord, help me to be faithful to you and to others.
Help me to keep my promises
and to be strong for those who depend on me.

Help me too, Lord, to be faith-full
to be filled with faith
so that I can rely on **your** promises
and **your** strength.

There are cracks and crevices in my life
where doubts and fears and weakness can slip in.
There are dark corners in me
where disbelief and distrust can hide.

FIll me to overflowing with faith, Lord,
a faith that leaves no room for doubt
no room for fear
no room for weakness.

Help me to be a faithful follower, Lord,
a faithful member of this choir
a faithful member of this congregation
and a believer filled to overflowing with faith.
Amen.

Feeling Like the Lone Ranger?

Scripture Reading: Psalm 102:1–2a, 6–7

Hear my prayer, O Lord; let my cry come to you. Do not hide your face from me in the day of my distress. I am like an owl of the wilderness, like a little owl of the waste places. I lie awake; I am like a lonely bird on the housetop.

Hymn Reference:
Blest Be the Tie That Binds   John Fawcett

Meditation:

Do you ever feel lonely?
Do you ever yearn for someone to talk to, **really** talk to?
Do you ever find yourself in a crowd and **still** feel alone?
Do you yearn for friendship?
for family?
for the feeling that your life counts for something important?
Do you struggle to fill your days?
your nights?
your calendar?

Take heart!
There are countless others who feel as you do . . .
who feel somehow disconnected from the hub of life.
There are countless others whose smiles cover their tears
whose laughter covers their emptiness
whose chatter covers their inner chasm.

Thank God for the church!
Thank God for the people of faith!
Thank God for a place
where we **can** be loved
where we **can** be important
where we **can** be connected.
Thank God for the church!

Reflection:

1. Sing the refrain of the hymn together. What is the hymn-writer's answer to believers who struggle with loneliness?

2. Some people are lonely because they live alone. Others are lonely because they feel alone no matter where they are. In what practical ways can the community of faith identify the lonely and address this very real need in society and in their midst?

3. In what practical ways can the choir and its ministry address the needs of the lonely members in the church and in the choir?

Prayer:

Lord,
you know what it is to be lonely.
We are Your people in this community of faith, Lord,
and many of us are lonely
even though it doesn't show.

Unite us in love, O Lord.
Let us not be afraid to show our true faces to one another.
Kindle the fires of compassion in us
so that we can reach out to our brothers and our sisters.
Free us from the bondage of our fears
and negative thoughts.
Break down the barriers that separate us from one another.
May we be a people committed to reaching out
committed to building bridges
committed to loving one another in Your name.
Amen.

Follow the Leader

Scripture Reading: Matthew 4:18–20

As he walked by the Sea of Galilee, he saw two brothers, Simon, who is called Peter, and Andrew his brother, casting a net into the sea—for they were fishermen. And he said to them, "Follow me, and I will make you fish for people." Immediately they left their nets and followed him.

Hymn Reference:

Dear Lord and Father of Mankind   John Greenleaf Whittier

Meditation:

It's hard to be a follower
when I would like to be a leader.

It's hard to let someone else take charge
when I could do it so much better.

It's hard to submit to someone else's agenda
when I have an agenda of my own.

It's hard to be a team player
when I know enough to be the Captain.

It's hard to listen to a sermon
when I could preach it better.

It's hard to be a choir member
when I am older and more experienced than the director.

It's hard to bend to God's will
when I'm so busy playing God myself.

Reflection:

1. Read the text or sing the hymn together. What does the hymnwriter say about our wilfulness as Christians?

2. Are you a good follower or do you always have to be the leader? If you have difficulty letting someone else be in charge, why do you think that is? Do you resent authority or do you genuinely believe you would be better at the task?

3. As a choir member how well do you do at trying to follow the leader's direction and interpretation of the music? As a Christian how well do you do at following God's direction for your life?

Prayer:

Forgiving God,
you know us so well.
You know how much each of us likes to be in charge.
We're more comfortable when we're in charge.
We're more secure when we're in charge.

But we cannot **always** be in charge.

Help us, O God, when we are called to follow, to do so
gracefully
willingly
joyfully.

As we learn to submit ourselves and our will to others
we will learn to submit ourselves and our will to You.
It will be a difficult but a good lesson for us, Lord.
Remind us that we still have a lot of learning to do.
Amen.

Forgiveness? For What?

Scripture Reading: Luke 23:34

Then Jesus said, "Father, forgive them; for they do not know what they are doing."

Hymn Reference:
There's a Wideness in God's Mercy   Frederick W. Faber

Meditation:

I am glad that I am not a sinner
at least not a **real** sinner.
I haven't done any **terrible** things.
I haven't murdered anyone
or **deliberately** hurt anyone.
I haven't lied
except when I **had** to.
I haven't cheated . . .
well, not in anything **really** important.
I go to church every Sunday
except when I've been out too late on Saturday.
I even sing in the choir
and I'm a pretty good singer too
not like that new person who just showed up for rehearsal.
I wonder what they're doing here.
They're certainly not good enough to sing in **this** group.

All things considered
I guess I'm a pretty good person
I'm thankful God can spend time on the really important things
and doesn't have to worry about me.

Reflection:

1. Sing or read the first three stanzas of the hymn. Is there anything in your life for which you would like to receive God's forgiveness? If so, allow the hymn to open the door to your honest confession and acceptance of God's grace.

2. Privately rate yourself on a scale of one to ten in terms of your personal level of righteousness. Do you make a distinction between "big" sins and "little" sins? If you were to ask the person who knows you the best, would they be likely to rate you as highly as you rated yourself?

3. Are you guilty as a choir member of any self-righteous attitudes? Do you welcome new singers? Are you guilty of considering yourself "one of the elite"?

Prayer:

Gracious and all-seeing God,
help us to see ourselves as You see us.
Help us to see ourselves as others see us.
Strip us of our pretenses.
Strip us of our disguises.
Strip us of all that keeps us from an honest relationship with You.
Amen.

Getting Away From It All

Scripture Reading: Psalm 139:7

Where can I go from your spirit? Or where can I flee from your presence?

Hymn Reference:
I Was There to Hear Your Borning Cry   John Ylvisaker

Meditation:

How many times have you heard someone say,
"I just need to get away from it all"?

How many times have **you** said
"I just need to get away from it all"?

What exactly is it that we need to get away **from?**
Work?
Family?
Pressures?
Debts?
Worries?
Responsibilities?

Yes, probably any one of those or all of them.

But maybe we are running from more than our problems.
Maybe we are trying to get away from **God.**
Maybe we are trying to get away from the **Holy Spirit.**

Maybe God is trying to get our attention
and we're not listening.
Maybe God is trying to help us deal with life
and we're trying to deal with it alone.
Maybe the weight of that
makes us want to get away from it all.

It's time to face the music!
There is no getting away from it all!
There is no getting away from God!
Let's stop running and start listening!

Reflection:

1. Sing the hymn or read the text together. How does this text comfort us?

2. Have you ever tried to get away from God? Can you share what happened in your life as a result?

3. Do you often feel you need to "get away from it all"? What hymn(s) are the most helpful to you when you feel the need to get away?

Prayer:

You were present, Lord, at my birth
and you will be present when my life ends.
You have been looking on and listening in
from the very beginning.
You have wept with me in my pain
and you have rejoiced in my victories.
You know me better than I know myself.

I know I cannot run from You.
I know I cannot hide from You.
But sometimes I forget.

When I think I need to get away from it all
what I really need is to stop running
and start listening!
Amen.

God of the Unexpected

Scripture Reading: Isaiah 43:19

I am about to do a new thing; now it springs forth, do you not perceive it?

Hymn Reference:

Lo! How a Rose E'er Blooming   German carol 16th c.

Meditation:

To be in the family of God can be an unnerving experience.
You never know what God will do next!
Our God is a God of surprises . . .
a God of thunderbolts and rainbows
a God of the unexpected.

Who would choose a stutterer to lead a nation?
Who would send a new baby home with geriatric parents?
Who would make an escape route in the middle of a vast body of water?
Who would send a small boy to fight a giant?
Who would cause a rose to bloom in the winter?
Who would send a baby to save the world?

Only a God of surprises!
Only a God of thunderbolts and rainbows!
Only a God of the unexpected!

Reflection:

1. Sing the hymn or read the text together. If you were to come upon a rose blooming in the midst of winter, how would you react? Would you believe it? Would you want to take it home to show others or would you leave it as an unexpected surprise for the next person? How does this familiar hymn give us an idea of what God is like?

2. Reflect for a moment on the story of Jesus' birth. Can you think of at least ten surprises in the way it all happened?

3. Have you ever had an experience where you have been surprised by God or become acutely aware of God's nature through an anthem or a hymn? Can you share your story with us?

Prayer:

O God of the unexpected
You have shown us in so many ways what You are like
in a world of infinite variety
in a universe with an extraordinary balance of order and chaos
in the way all creatures are different . . . and alike
in the unfolding of Your story from Genesis to Revelation
in the willingness to send Your only Son to fulfill a promise.

You have shown us in so many ways what You are like
and though we can never quite know You
help us to know You well enough
to always expect
the impossible
the radical
the surprising
the unexpected.
Amen.

47

God Present in Us

Scripture Reading: Luke 4:18a

The Spirit of the Lord is upon me.

Hymn Reference:
Like the Murmur of the Dove's Song   Carl P. Daw, Jr.

Meditation:

God's Spirit is truly present
around us
with us
in us.

In truth and in tenderness
in healing and in harmony
in welcome and in wisdom
in love and in laughter
in song and in silence
in justice and in joy
in peace and in power
in comfort and in counsel
in mystery and in music.

God's Spirit is truly present
around us
with us
in us.
Thanks be to God!

Reflection:

1. Sing the hymn or read the text together. What are some of the powerful images the hymnwriter employs to help us understand the nature of the Holy Spirit and its work among us?

2. There are many ways in which the Holy Spirit has been described. What image is the most appealing for you?

3. Have you been aware of the working of the Holy Spirit in your own life? Can you share your experience?

Prayer:

O God,
the Holy Spirit,
come to us, and be among us;

Come as the wind and cleanse us.
Come as the fire and burn away the chaff.
Come as the dew and refresh our spirits.

Convict
convert
and consecrate our hearts
and our lives
and our voices
to our great good
and to Your greater glory.
Amen.
(Adapted from an Anonymous prayer)

The Great Commission

Scripture Reading: Mark 16:15

And he said to them, "Go into all the world and proclaim the good news to the whole creation."

Hymn Reference:
Lord, You Give the Great Commission   Jeffrey Rowthorn

Meditation:

Jesus did indeed give us the great commission.
He asked us to spread the good news of the gospel wherever we can . . .
to heal the sick
to witness in word and song
to practice forgiveness
to share our gifts freely
in short, to serve . . .
to live His life on earth.

Well, it's not as easy as it sounds!

It's hard to get caught up in a heavenly mission
when our hardened hearts
and our muddled minds
are focused on earthly things.

But that's not what God intended.

From the very beginning in the Garden of Eden
God used earthly beauty to give us a glimpse of heaven.

From the very beginning
God employed the tangible
to help us grasp the intangible.

From the very beginning
God employed the common
to help us get in touch with the holy.

If we are earthbound
unable to get caught up in our heavenly mission
we have only ourselves to blame.
We have set our sights on the gifts
and forgotten to look beyond them to the Giver.

Reflection:

1. Sing the hymn or read the text together. What do you think the hymnwriter means by the phrase "life abundant meant for each"?

2. Does singing in the choir help you to fulfill the Great Commission? If so, in what ways?

3. Can you think of some common things that God makes holy?

Prayer:

Lord of the common
God of the holy
You have called us into Your service.
Let us joyfully answer that call.
Let us be caught up in Your heavenly mission.
Tune our hearts and our voices to sing out the good news.
Let us
each one
take the Great Commission seriously.
Loose the bonds that hold us captive here on earth.
Set our eyes and our hearts and our song on things eternal
for Your sake.
Amen.

I Don't Have Time to Pray!

Scripture Reading: I Thessalonians 5:17

Pray without ceasing.

Hymn Reference:
Take Time to be Holy   William Longstaff

Meditation:

Don't ask me to pray!
I don't have time.
Can't you see how busy I am?

There are bills to pay and promises to keep
people to see and problems to solve
birthdays to celebrate and deaths to mourn.
My children are growing up and my parents are growing old.
Somehow hope has slipped out of my days and fear had crept into my nights
I'm overextended and underpaid.
I'm in debt and out of control.
I'm struggling to lose weight and I'm desperate to find peace.

Don't ask me to pray!
I don't have time.
Can't you see how busy I am?
Can't you see how frightened I am?
Can't you see how needy I am?
Don't ask me to pray!
I don't have time.

Reflection:

1. Read the hymn text aloud. What are the ways in which this hymn text speaks to your personal situation?

2. Can you think of some ways to find time to pray in spite of a hectic schedule?

3. Do you think it's possible to pray and sing at the same time? Is there a hymn or an anthem that could be a prayer for you when you sing it?

Prayer:

Lord, we know we need to visit with You more often.
We have so much we need to tell You.
There must be things You want to tell us too
but we always seem to be too busy to listen.
Help us to find time for You.
Help us to find time for ourselves.

Help us to see that we're not too busy to pray.
Help us to see that we're too busy not to pray.

Amen.

Is This My Father's World?

Scripture Reading: Psalm 24:1–2

The earth is the Lord's and all that is in it, the world and those who live in it, for he founded it on the seas, and established it on the rivers.

Hymn Reference:
This Is My Father's World   Maltbie D. Babcock

Meditation:

Is this my Father's world?
If it is why isn't all nature singing?

It seems as if the beauty
and music
and glory
of God's creation
is slipping through our fingers.

The beauty of the morning is not what it once was.
The birds' carols are drowned out
by the roar of heavy equipment.
We call it progress.
The lilies struggle to lift their faces to the sun.
The rustling grass has become a patch of concrete.
The skies are ripe with unseen particles,
terrible and toxic.
The seas have issued a warning.
The rocks and trees cry out for us to notice.

Is this my Father's world?
If it is, why isn't all nature singing?

Reflection:

1. Read the text of the hymn together. What are three central themes in the hymnwriter's text?

2. What are the signs in nature that confirm God's presence and power for you?

3. What is our responsibility as Christians to this planet and to God's creation?

Prayer:

Lord, we have not cared for Your world as we should.
We have not protected Your world as we should.
We have not loved Your creatures and Your creation as we should.

Open our eyes, Lord.
Help us to see what is happening to Your world and to us.
Open our ears, Lord.
Help us to hear what is happening to Your world and to us
Open our hearts, Lord.
Help us to feel what is happening to Your world and to us.

Forgive us, Lord, for careless and greedy ways.
Forgive us for wasting Your precious gifts
Give us courage, Lord,
to speak
to act
to change
before it is too late.

Amen.

I've Got a Secret!

Scripture Reading: Numbers 32:23b

. . . and be sure your sin will find you out!

Hymn Reference:
O For a Thousand Tongues to Sing   Charles Wesley

Meditation:

As soon as we are old enough
to know the difference between right and wrong
we are old enough to begin keeping secrets.
But secrets are **hard** to keep as we all know.
They **beg** to be told.
They **beg** to be shared.
They **beg** to be **exposed** to the light.
It is a kind of two-edged sword.
We act in ways that **require** us to keep secrets
but we are **driven** to confess them to someone
to anyone who will listen
because the weight of them is too heavy to carry.

By tradition, the church has always been the place to go
to tell your secrets
and to be absolved of them.
But what about all of the people who are not believers?
What about those who have nothing to do with the church?
What can **they** do to be rid of their troubling secrets?
How can they get them off their conscience?

Society would have us believe
that technology has all the answers.
So, today we can turn on the television
to any number of exposé type talk shows
where individuals can tell their secrets to a **live** studio audience
and to millions of other viewers around the country
who seem to love to look in
on the very private and sordid lives of their fellow Americans.

We have in effect replaced the altar rail
the confessional booth
the priest
and ultimately God as well
with a camera and cable television access.
What can we be thinking?
Yes, we **can** confess our most outrageous secrets to millions
and perhaps even feel a certain sense of relief in the telling
but the television viewers cannot forgive our sins!
They cannot liberate us or grant us **new** life!
God and God alone
has the power to grant us those extraordinary gifts of grace.

Reflection:

1. Sing the hymn or read the text together. What does the hymn writer tell us about God's power in relation to our sin?

2. Some have described this new talk show phenomenon as "silly", a "cultural cartoon" not meant to be taken seriously. What do you think these shows tell us about ourselves?

3. If the members of the choir were to know any of **your** secrets, how would they react. . . . Would they gossip? Would they judge you or would they pray for you?

Prayer:

O God
You alone know all of our secrets
and You alone have the power to forgive them
to erase them as if they had never happened.
Help us to readily confess our secrets to You
and to joyfully accept the gift of Your unlimited forgiveness.
Amen.

Joy to the World!

Scripture Reading: Isaiah 9:6–7

For a child has been born for us, a son given to us; authority rests upon his shoulders; and he is named Wonderful Counselor, Mighty God, Everlasting Father, Price of Peace.

His authority shall grow continually, and there shall be endless peace for the throne of David and his kingdom. He will establish it and uphold it with justice and righteousness from this time onward and forevermore.

Hymn Reference:

Joy to the World! Isaac Watts
adapt. from Psalm 98

Meditation:

Suddenly it's **Christmas morning!**
There is welcome and joy in the air
and the glad sound of angels' singing.

We race down the stairs and out to the barn.
And now
breathless
we stand beside the manger.
You are here, Lord!
You are here at last!

After **all** that waiting
after **all** that preparation
after **all** that worrying
you are really finally truly here
snuggling deep into Your mother's arms
curling Your tiny fingers around hers
tugging at the heartstrings of the world.

And now
in the measured silence of a winter morning
in the radiant presence of God's gift
to a weary and trembling world
we realize that **this** is what Advent is all about
excited
joyous
eager anticipation
and
at last
welcome!

Reflection:

1. Read the text or sing the hymn together. Why do you think this particular hymn is such a favorite choice for Christmas morning or Christmas Sunday?

2. Do you still have enthusiasm as you approach Christmas or are there things about the season that sap your energy and your joy? What could make Christmas a more joyous occasion for you?

3. It may be that the choir and the musicians of the church begin preparing for the Christmas season earlier than anyone else in the church. Do you make any **spiritual** preparations for Christmas as a choir or as an individual?

Prayer:

We welcome You to this world, Lord.
We have been anxiously waiting for You to arrive.
We have read the promises
and we know that Your coming
means that there **is** hope for us
that peace **is** possible
and that justice **can** be a reality.

Joy to the World!
Amen.

The Last Word

Scripture Reading: Revelation 2:10b

Be faithful until death and I will give you the crown of life.

Hymn Reference:
Soon and Very Soon Andraé Crouch

Meditation:

Someone I know passed away recently.
He was a Christian, one of God's saints.
When we remember him,
what will we say about him?
What will his family say about him?
What will his obituary say?

When we have breathed **our** last breath
all that will be left to remember us
is family
and friends
the work we have done
the lives we have touched.
And in the end
it will all come down to a brief summary
a few lines of conversation
a few lines in the paper
a few lines in a family history
a few lines carved in stone.

How would I summarize my life
my contribution
my place in my family
my place in history?

Reflection:

1. Sing the hymn together. For the Christian, death is an affirmation of all that we have believed, all that we have lived for. Is this hymn an affirmation of your life?

2. If you were to write your own obituary, what would you like it to say?

3. When you are gone, what would you hope your friends and family would remember most about you? What would you hope the choir would remember?

Prayer:

O God of our first breath
and God of our last,
You alone know how many days have been allotted to us.
You alone know how we spend our precious minutes and hours.
Grant us a clear vision of what it is that we truly value
and help us to free ourselves
from all those things that would waste our time
our talent
and our resources.
Help us to give our lives over to You
and to others in Your name.

Let us be remembered for our willing spirit
for our loving care of others
and for our joyful song.
Amen.

Lent Is Not My Favorite Time of Year!

Scripture Reading: John 3:16

For God so loved the world that He gave His only begotten Son that whosoever believeth in him should not perish but have eternal life.

Hymn Reference:
When I Survey the Wondrous Cross   Isaac Watts

Meditation:

I have a confession to make.
Lent is not my favorite time of year.
It's such a dreary time.
And the music is especially unappealing.
The songs are sad
and they all seem to be in minor keys
and the words are all about death and blood and sacrifice
and things that make me feel bad.
I don't go to church to feel bad.
I go to church to feel better.

It's not as if I don't really care about Jesus' sacrifice.
But that **was** a long time ago
and the notion of Lent just doesn't grab me
if you know what I mean.
What do ashes and penance and sacrifice have to do with me?
Those things are for people who have no real life.

I like Palm Sunday and Easter.
The music is loud and the message is upbeat
and I don't have to deal with gloom and doom.

Yes, to be brutally honest,
Lent is not my favorite time of year.

Reflection:

1. Sing the hymn or read the text together. What is most positive in this Lenten text? Would you classify this as a "gloom and doom" Lenten hymn? Why or why not?

2. If you are like many, you do not enjoy the season of Lent. Why do you think we should celebrate the season at all?

3. Is there something you or your choir or your church could do to make the celebration of Lent something more than an unpleasant duty?

Prayer:

When we finally stop complaining, Lord,
and allow the silence to settle around us
perhaps we might catch a glimpse
just a glimpse
of what Lent is all about.

It's about hearing the story again
for the very first time.
It's about walking where You walked.
It's about touching Your robe
and feeling Your power surge through us.
It's about feeling Your fear and Your pain on the cross
and knowing it was for us You died.
It's about basking in the sunshine
of Your love and forgiveness.
It's about holding out our empty hands
and receiving the costly and generous gift
of Your amazing grace.

Perhaps if we make a real effort to see the bigger picture
Lent just might become our favorite time of year.
Amen and Amen.

Life in the City

Scripture Reading: Matthew 11:20

Then he began to reproach the cities in which most of his deeds of power had been done, because they did not repent.

Hymn Reference:
Where Cross the Crowded Ways of Life   Frank M. North

Meditation:

If Christ were to walk the city streets today
what would He see?
What would He hear?
What would He think of it all?

Would He find our lives crowded?
Would He find crowded streets
crowded stores
crowded calendars
crowded minds?

Would He find "wretchedness and need"
on streetcorners
in alleys
in parks
and in plazas?

Would He watch "restless throngs"
hurrying to work
hurrying home
hurrying to and from appointments,
hurrying to fill the spaces in empty lives?

Would He hear racial slurs
spilling out of the ghettos
into streets and suburbs
spilling out of the hearts of the oppressed
the hopeless
the hungry?

Would He hear on every side
the "noise of selfish strife"
blaring horns
angry voices
frenzied music?

If Christ were to walk the city streets today
what would He think of it all?

Reflection:

1. Sing the hymn or read the text together. What images in the text hit you the hardest? Note that the original text was written in 1903. Does the message still seem relevant today?

2. If you were to walk the streets of your own city today, would you see and hear the kinds of things the textwriter talked about? If not, how does your city differ? What could make all cities more humane, more joyful, more welcoming?

3. What impact do you think "frenzied music" has on community life? on your own life?

Prayer:

Lord, go with us into the streets of our city.
Help us to see our communal lives through Your eyes.
Lay a burden on our hearts for those who suffer in the city
from hunger, need, overcrowding and hopelessness.
Above all of the noise of the city, Lord,
let us hear Your voice
and catch the vision of Your tears.
Amen.

Life in Three Dimensions

Scripture Reading: John 14:19b

Because I live, you also will live.

Hymn Reference:
Because He Lives   Gloria Gaither and William Gaither

Meditation:

The future is just around the corner.
Tomorrow, next week, next month, next year . . .
they are all part of the future.

Some of us live in the future every day . . .
waiting for things to get better
waiting for the next paycheck
waiting for the car to be paid off
waiting for the kids to get in school
waiting for the kids to get out of college.
Somehow we use up the present by focusing our attention on the future.

Some of us live in the past . . .
trying to get over old hurts
trying to get rid of old grievances
trying to heal from old wounds.
We use up the present by focusing our attention on what is past.

But those of us who are Easter People
who are made new by Jesus' death and resurrection
have the unique opportunity to be in three dimensions at once.

We rejoice daily in the past
grateful that it is behind us
grateful that our sins are forgiven and forgotten
grateful for new life in Christ.
God has forgiven the past!

We rejoice daily in the future
grateful that our future is in God's hands
grateful that we don't have to fret over tomorrow
or what tomorrow holds
God holds the future!

And we Easter People rejoice daily in the present moment
grateful for what is right now
grateful that God walks beside us
walks with us
lives in us.
God owns the present!

Alleluia!

Reflection:

1.   Sing the hymn or read the text together. This song is pure gospel. What is the greatest affirmation for you personally in the text?

2.   Do you live in the past? Do you worry about the future? Or are you truly an Easter Person?

3.   Can you think of a hymn or chorus that reinforces your commitment to be an Easter Person?

Prayer:

O God of the Empty Tomb
You are the one true God.
You are God of the past, of the present and the future.
Help me to trust You with all the dimensions of my life.
Amen.

Living in Common Time

Scripture Reading: Ecclesiastes 3:1-8

For everything there is a season, and a time for every matter under heaven: a time to be born and a time to die; a time to plant, and a time to pluck up what is planted; a time to kill, and a time to heal; a time to break down and a time to build up; a time to weep, and a time to laugh; a time to mourn, and a time to dance; a time to throw away stones, and a time to gather stones together; a time to embrace, and a time to refrain from embracing; a time to seek, and a time to lose; a time to keep, and a time to speak; a time to love, and a time to hate; a time for war, and a time for peace.

Hymn Reference:

In the Bulb There Is a Flower   Natalie Sleeth

Meditation:

We live in common time.

What binds us together as community
is what we share in common . . .
what we celebrate and what we mourn
what we seek and what we fear
the victories and the disappointments
the laughter and the tears
the songs and the silences
the seasons of our lives.

And
at the heart of it all
is
the God who made us . . .
each one unique
each one individual
each one lovingly crafted
designed to live in community with others
designed to experience life with others
designed to live in common time.

Reflection:

1. Sing the hymn together. What does the hymn say to you about what all human beings share in common?

2. What are the things, the commonalities, that Christians share?

3. How do the songs of our faith help us to live in common time?

Prayer:

Lord
help me to live in common time
with my brothers and sisters
in this church
in this community
in this world
in this age.

Let me rejoice with those who rejoice
and weep with those who weep.

Let me love all children as my own.
Let me care for all the afflicted as my own.
Let me share the blessings and bereavements
of all your children.

Lord
let me live in common time.
Amen.

Make a List!

Scripture Reading: Psalm 66:5

Come and see what God has done: he is awesome in his deeds among mortals.

Hymn Reference:

I Sing the Mighty Power of God   Isaac Watts
tr. John M. Neale, 1851; st. 5 Henry Sloane Coffin, 1916

Meditation:

There is **one** thing I am really good at.
I am good at forgetting things.
I forget what I was going to get at the store.
I forget to take the library books back.
I forget to pay the bills on time.
I could forget almost anything if I didn't make a list.

Sometimes I even forget how big God really is.
Sometimes I forget how lavish He is with His blessings.
Sometimes I forget how much beauty and diversity
He has provided in this world.

What power!
What imagination!
What style!

Funny! I can remember so many unnecessary things
old lovers
old grievances
old addresses.

How can I so easily forget the really important things?
How can I forget how big God really is?

Reflection:

1. Sing the hymn or read the text together. What specific things does the hymnwriter name that remind him of how big God is?

2. When the Jews celebrate Seder they recite the list of God's mighty acts in their history. It is a way of reminding themselves as a community of how God has cared for them. Make a list of the things God has done in your life and in the lives of those you know.

3. What hymn or anthem best expresses God's power for you?

Prayer:

Jog my memory, Lord.
Help me to remember the things that really count.
Help me to remember that You are a big God
bigger than I can even imagine.
Help me to remember the most important thing of all:
You are not too big to remember me!
Amen.

Meditation on a Mystery

Scripture Reading: John 13:7

Jesus answered, "You do not know now what I am doing, but later you will understand."

Hymn Reference:
God Moves in a Mysterious Way   William Cowper

Meditation:

I love a good mystery.
Part of the fun is to try to guess how it will end.
Sometimes, If I can't stand the suspense,
I sneak a peek at the last few pages.
Sometimes . . . but hardly ever.
It's nice to know that I can.

But life is something else again . . .
one big mystery and no way to jump ahead
no way to peek at the ending
even though I might like to
even though I might **need** to.

I guess I'm one of those "fearful saints"
the hymnwriter talks about
afraid of how things **might** turn out,
always expecting rain instead of blessing
always dreading instead of anticipating.
I'm one of those impatient believers
wanting my prayers answered **now**
wanting to enjoy the flower
before the bud has had a chance to open.

Why can't I just relax and enjoy the mystery
the ultimate and beautiful mystery
of God's presence in my life?
I don't have to know how it will turn out.
Not really.
As long as **He** knows the ending
I can just keep turning the pages.

Reflection:

1. Sing the hymn or read the text together. What examples does the hymnwriter employ to tell us how God works?

2. What was one of the most difficult times in **your** life when you wanted to jump ahead and find out how things would turn out? Looking back now, would it have helped if you had known the ending or was it ultimately better not to know?

3. What parallels do you see between the believer's relationship with God and the choir's relationship with the director?

Prayer:

Lord, why do You have to be so mysterious?
Why do You allow us to grope around in the dark
when a single word from You could light up the room?
Why do You allow us to tremble with fear
when a single word from You could calm our anxiety?
Why do You take so long to answer our prayers
when You could answer them in a heartbeat?

There's no denying it, Lord.
Most of us are fearful and impatient believers.
We want to know how things will turn out
and we want to know **now**.

Show us how to trust You more.
Show us how to wait on You.
Teach us how to enjoy just turning pages.
Amen.

Music: a Fair and Glorious Gift

Scripture Reading: Psalm 100:1–2

*Make a joyful noise to the Lord, all the earth. Worship the Lord with glad-
ness. Come into his presence with singing.*

Hymn Reference:

Come, Christians, Join to Sing   Christian Henry Bateman

Meditation:

Martin Luther said:

I wish to see all arts
principally music
in the service of Him who gave and created them.

Music is a fair and glorious gift of God.

I would not for the world
forego my humble share of music.

Singers are never sorrowful, but are merry
and smile through their troubles in song.
Music makes people kinder, gentler, more staid and reasonable.

I am strongly persuaded that after theology
there is no art that can be placed on a level with music;
for besides theology
music is the only art capable of affording peace and joy of the heart.
The devil flees before the sound of music
almost as much as before the Word of God.

Reflection:

1. How does music differ from the other arts? What is unique about music?

2. How do you feel about the place of music in worship . . . its impact, its power to present the gospel message, its importance as a corporate act?

3. The author of this hymn text sees singing for the Christian as an act of praise. Sing each line of the hymn antiphonally and let it be an act of praise for you.

Prayer:

How good it is, Lord, to join with other voices in song
to celebrate your mighty acts
to remember our past
to reaffirm our faith
to rejoice in our future
to mourn those who are no longer with us.

There are times when the power and beauty of song
makes us tremble.

There are times when it seems
we can hardly endure the joy of a song heartily sung
or the pain of a song offered in loving remembrance
of one no longer present with us.

But this we know, Lord,
when we come into Your presence with a song
we are reminded in a mighty way
of how glorious and powerful a gift we share.
Amen.

A Nasty Surprise

Scripture Reading: Mark 14:18b

Truly I tell you, one of you will betray me, one who is eating with me.

Hymn Reference:
'Tis Midnight; and on Olive's Brow   William B. Tappan

Meditation:

To be betrayed is bad enough.
To be betrayed by someone close to you
by someone trusted
by someone loved
is worse.
It is at best a nasty surprise!

Who among us has not encountered this kind of betrayal?
Husband
Wife
Child
Parent
Pastor
Employer
Best Friend

Who among us is able to forgive it?
Who among us is able to easily trust again?
Who among us is able to close the wound?

Christ lived his life on earth
and encountered the best and worst of what we are about.
And unlike us
He **knew** He would be betrayed
and He lived with that
and was even able to forgive those who betrayed Him.

Who is vulnerable?
Anyone who invests herself in life.
Anyone who invests himself in others.
Anyone who invests herself in the church.
Anyone who invests himself in the choir.
And there is nothing to do with the anger and pain of it
but to forgive.

Reflection:

1. Sing the hymn or read the text together. Notice how the author points up Jesus' ultimate loneliness. Jesus knew he would be betrayed. The hymnwriter gives a good picture of how painful betrayal is. How do you respond to the message of this hymn?

2. Have you ever been betrayed by someone close to you? How did it feel? Did you confront them? Were you ever able to forgive them?

3. How can you allow yourself to become vulnerable again once you have been betrayed? How can you protect yourself without becoming a lonely and bitter person?

Prayer:

Lord Jesus
You suffered the ultimate betrayal.
You can understand the pain we feel when we have been betrayed.
You can understand the pain we feel
when we have given our lives and our talents to a family
to a career
to a church
to a choir
and have been cast aside.

Where we are wounded help us to heal.
Where we are angry help us to forgive.
Where we are distrustful help us to regain our faith.
Amen.

A New Perspective on Servanthood

Scripture Reading: I Corinthians 7:22b (KJV)

. . . likewise also he that is called, being free, is Christ's servant.

Hymn Reference:
Christ Has No Hands but Our Hands   Mary Kay Beall
See Appendix page 140

Meditation:

In a London church known as St. Martin's-in-the-Field
there is a sign which reads:

"A Christian is a mind through which Christ thinks:
a heart through which Christ loves,
a voice through which Christ speaks,
a hand through which Christ helps."

C. S. Lewis says that we Christians are "mirrors"
"carriers" of Christ to others
that
"our real selves are all waiting for us in Him."

Christ has no body now on earth but yours.
Yours are the only hands with which He can do His work.
Yours are the only feet with which He can go about the world.
Yours are the only eyes through which His compassion can shine
upon a troubled world.

Christ has no body now on earth but yours.

Reflection:

1. Read the text of the hymn. Do you allow Christ to use your hands, your feet, your arms, your heart and your voice to do His work in the world?

2. How do you view **your** ministry in the choir? Why are **you** here? What is the choir's ultimate function in the church? Does this choir have a sense of ministry as a foundation for their service?

3. How could **you** be a better "voice" for Christ?

Prayer:

Lord,
when You lived on this earth
You showed us what it meant to be a servant.

Remind us of the ways in which You served those You met.
Remind us that serving others is at the heart of Your message.
Remind us that passive Christianity is not what You had in mind.
Help us to be Your willing servants in this world
in this community
in this church
in this choir.
Amen.

Paying Tribute

Scripture Reading: Psalm 113:1–3, 9b

Praise the Lord! Praise, O servants of the Lord; praise the name of the Lord. Blessed be the name of the Lord from this time on and forevermore. From the rising of the sun to its setting, the name of the Lord is to be praised. Praise the Lord!

Hymn Reference:

My Tribute   Andraé Crouch

Meditation:

My song is my offering.
It is not much I know
in comparison with what I have received.
And yet it is an intimate
and vital part of who I am.

My voice is not the voice of an angel.
It is in many ways an average voice.
Sometimes I sing out of tune.
Sometimes I am afraid to sing out.
But I am always thankful for a voice
to sing God's praise.

I thank God for the gift of song
and I thank God for the gracious gift of music.
When I sing
I find joy
and peace
and fulfillment
even when my song is imperfect.

My song is my offering
and I offer it with a grateful and willing heart.

Reflection:

1. Read the hymn text aloud. Sing the hymn. How does singing the text increase the power of the message?

2. How would your life be different if you could not sing? How would your church be different if there were no choir?

3. If you could only sing one hymn or anthem as your song offering to God, what would you choose to sing?

Prayer:

If my lips could sing as many songs
as there are waves in the sea;
if my tongue could sing as many hymns
as there are ocean billows;
if my mouth filled the whole firmament with praise;
if my face shone like the sun and moon together;
if my hands were to hover in the sky like powerful eagles
and my feet ran across mountains as swiftly as the deer;
all that would not be enough to pay you fitting tribute,
O Lord my God.
Amen and Amen.
(Hymn probably composed in the Talmudic period, 3rd–5th century A.D.)

Plenty to Eat and Going Hungry!

Scripture Reading: Psalm 107:9

For he satisfies the thirsty, and the hungry he fills with good things.

Hymn Reference:
Fill My Cup, Lord   Richard Blanchard

Meditation:

We are hungry, Lord.
We have more than enough to eat.
Some of us could even stand to lose a few pounds.
But yes, we are **hungry!**

We are hungry for something more than church membership.
We are hungry for something more than platitudes.
We are hungry for something more than casual friendships.
We are hungry for something more than great ideas
and stimulating conversation.
We are hungry for something more than money and pleasure.

What is it that keeps us from being satisfied?
What is it that keeps us lonely in a crowd?
What is it that keeps us greedy and distracted?

We have so much
so many **things**
but deep down inside there is an empty place
a place that money and possessions and achievements cannot satisfy.
What is missing in our lives?
What would it take to keep us from being hungry?

Reflection:

1. Sing the hymn or read the text together. What does the song tell us we need to be satisfied?

2. Do you feel satisfied in your daily life? Do you feel satisfied in your spiritual life? What are the things that you hunger for?

3. As a choir member you give a good bit of yourself and your time and talent to the choir? Do you feel satisfied with what you receive from this commitment? If not, what would make it more satisfying?

Prayer:

Lord, You know that we are hungry.
And You know what it is that we hunger for.

We need Your power and presence and healing in our lives.
We need Your song and Your joy in our hearts.
We need to hear Your word and to do Your will.
We need friends who truly love us and care for us
friends who are in touch with You
friends who are alive with Your indwelling

Lord, You know that we are hungry.
And You know what it is that we hunger for.
Feed us, Lord.
Satisfy our hungry hearts.
Amen.

Praise Is a State of Mind

Scripture Reading: Psalm 146:1–2

Praise the Lord! Praise the Lord, O my soul! I will praise the Lord as long as I live; I will sing praises to my God all my life long!

Hymn Reference:

I'll Praise My Maker Isaac Watts
adapt. by John Wesley

Meditation:

Praise the Lord?
Some days that's hard to do.
Some days I look at my life
and all I can see is the dark side:
habits I can't seem to break
angers I can't let go of
opportunities I've lost
frustrations at work
worries about my health.

To be honest
some days all I can see are the unanswered prayers
clustered in the corners of my life
like dustballs
and I don't feel like praising the Lord.

I **want** to believe.
I **want** to be grateful
but some days I'm just too busy sighing.

How can I **feel** like praising?
What has God done for **me** lately?
What prayers have actually been answered?
What burdens have become lighter?
What miracles can I rejoice in?

When?
Tell me **when** God is going to do something for **me**
something worthy of praise?

Reflection:

1. Sing the hymn or read the text together. What is the text writer's attitude about giving praise to God?

2. How do you feel toward God today? Do you feel like praising or are you holding off praising God until He does something real in your life?

3. One of the ways Christians offer praise to God is through their singing. What hymn or anthem is your favorite avenue for praising God?

Prayer:

Merciful and Loving God,
forgive us for our unwillingness to praise You as we should.
Some days
it's a wonder You don't give up on us.

Who do we think we are
wanting You to jump through **our** hoop
before we are willing to reward **You** with our praise?

As your children
we are to praise You for **who** You are
not just for **what** You do!

Remind me, O God, that praise is not a conditional response.
Praise is a state of mind.
Amen.

Prepare the Way!

Scripture Reading: Isaiah 40:3, 5

A voice cries out: "In the wilderness prepare the way of the Lord, make straight in the desert a highway for our God."

Then the glory of the Lord shall be revealed and all people shall see it together, for the mouth of the Lord has spoken.

Hymn Reference:
Come, Thou Long-Expected Jesus   Charles Wesley

Meditation:

In the crisp chill of a fall morning,
we hear the prophet cry out,
"Prepare the way of the Lord!"
His voice booms over the hillside like a cannon
and echos across the wide valley.

Every day now we will look for Your coming . . .
eager . . . trembling with anticipation.
Every day now we will watch the sky
to see if the star has appeared.

Soon we will be too excited to sleep.
We'll run outside to the barn to scoop up the hay.
We'll find the empty manger.
We'll prop the barn door open
so You will know You are welcome here.
And then . . .
And then we will lay awake . . . taut . . . listening . . .
anxious for the first gentle sound of Your coming.

Reflection:

1. Sing the hymn. What mood does the hymn create for you? What line in the text best captures your idea of who Jesus is . . . or the reason for His coming?

2. The meditation captures a child's reaction to the news of Christ's coming. Do you feel excited each year when the season of Advent begins? How can you grab hold of a child's excitement and make Advent a fresh, new experience this year?

3. What can **you** do . . . what can **this** choir do . . . to prepare the way?

Prayer:

O God
to whom a thousand years is but a day
we confess to You
that we are impatient creatures,
We are not good at waiting for things.
We are not good at delays.
If we had our way
we would just jump into Christmas Eve
and get on with the story.

But You are a God of endless patience
and You know that waiting can be a good thing.

Help us to learn that lesson.
Let us learn to use this time of waiting
to prepare the way
to prepare a place for the Child to be born . . .
a place in our own impatient and eager hearts.
Amen.

Professing Our Faith

Scripture Reading: Philippians 2:11

> . . . *every tongue should confess that Jesus Christ is Lord, to the glory of God the father.*

Hymn Reference:

He Is Lord   Anon.

Meditation:

How often do **you** profess your faith.
Every day in your daily meditations?
Every Sunday in your worship?
Now and then in worship?
Never?

Consider this.
Every time you gather for rehearsal
every time you gather for worship
every time you sing the hymns of the faith
every time you sing an anthem or a response
you are, in fact, professing your faith
in the One in whom you believe
in the One in whom you place your trust
in the One who gave His life for you
in the One who gave you the gift of music to share.

No, it is not a formal affirmation.
It is not a formal profession.
It is not a traditional creed.
And yet our song is an honest expression of what we believe.
Whether we sing a hymn
or the sacred music of the Renaissance
whether we sing Bach or a traditional anthem
whether we sing a new musical creation or a praise chorus
if the text glorifies God and God's word to all of us
it is indeed our own profession of faith.
It is our credo in song.

Reflection:

1. Do you think about the text of the music you sing as a choir? Do you think about the text of each hymn in the worship service and what it has to do with the message? Do you ever think about the message of the anthem? Do you believe what you sing?

2. Can you think of the text of a hymn or an anthem that is a true profession of your faith or that connects with your own faith journey? Will you share that text with us?

3. Sing the hymn together. Are these words a good profession of what **you** believe?

Prayer:

Hear us now, Lord, as we profess our faith.
(Read the Ecum. version of the Apostles' Creed together
from your hymnal or from a printed copy.)

I believe in God, the Father almighty, creator of heaven and earth.
I believe in Jesus Christ, God's only Son, our Lord,
who was conceived by the Holy Spirit,
born of the Virgin Mary,
suffered under Pontius Pilate,
was crucified, died, and was buried;
he descended to the dead.
On the third day he rose again;
he ascended into heaven,
is seated at the right hand of the Father,
and will come to judge the living and the dead.
I believe in the Holy Spirit
the holy catholic church
the communion of saints
the forgiveness of sins
the resurrection of the body
and the life everlasting.
Amen.

A Psalm for the Choir

Scripture Reading: Psalm 15

O Lord, who may abide in your tent? Who may dwell on your holy hill?

Those who walk blamelessly, and do what is right and speak the truth from their heart.
  who do not slander with their tongue and do not evil to their friends
  nor take up a reproach against their neighbors;
  in whose eyes the wicked are despised, but who honor those who fear the Lord.
  who stand by their oath even to their hurt, who do not lend money at interest
  and do not take a bribe against the innocent.

Those who do these things shall never be moved.

Hymn Reference:
Rejoice, You Pure in Heart   Edward H. Plumptre

Meditation:

O Lord, who may abide in your choir?
Who may sit in that holy loft?

Those who sing blamelessly
and do what is right
and enunciate the text clearly and from their heart.

Who do not slander the director with their tongues
and do no evil to the other singers
nor take up a reproach against any soloist;

In whose eyes unfaithfulness is despised,
who honor the director and respect the other singers
who give their best efforts even when the rehearsal runs over
who do not lend music nor misplace it
and who do not blame their own mistakes on the innocent.

Those who do these things shall never be moved!

Reflection:

1. Sing or read the hymn together, stanzas 1–4. What does the hymnwriter have to say about singers in the church?

2. Look around you at the other members of the choir. Does this group reflect diversity? . . . in the hymnwriter's words . . . "Bright youth and snow-crowned age, strong souls and spirits meek"? If you would like a more diverse membership how would you go about attracting new members?

3. The **choir** version of Psalm 15 takes a somewhat humorous look at what makes a good choir member. What do **you** think makes a good choir member? Does your description fit you?

Prayer:

Make me a good choir member, Lord.

Help me to always do my best at all times.
Help me to be a positive influence in this group
to be faithful in attendance
to follow the director's leadership
to respect the other singers
even the uncertain singers
to take responsibility for my own music and materials
and to never blame my mistakes on others.

Make me a good choir member, Lord.
Amen!

Put Your Whole Self In

Scripture Reading: Colossians 3:23

Whatever your task, put yourselves into it, as done for the Lord . . .

Hymn Reference:
Take My Life and Let It Be   Frances Havergal

Meditation:

Years ago there was a popular dance called the Hokey Pokey.
One of the lines in the song was an exhortation to
"Put your whole self in".
Those of us who are old enough to remember the dance
remember jumping with great enthusiasm into the circle on that line.

When we were young it was easy to put our whole selves in.
It's too bad we have so much trouble doing that today.
Maybe growing older saps our enthusiasm
or maybe we just become wary.
People who put their whole selves in
tend to look a little over zealous.
Today, the style is to be "laid back", to be reserved.

People who put their whole selves in
make the rest of us look bad.
They go at full speed.
By comparison, **we** seem to be moving in slow motion.
So . . . we hardly ever put our whole selves in!

But that's exactly what Christ calls us to do.
To give our whole selves over to His agenda.
To put our whole selves into the new life He offers.
To put our whole selves into a new way of being.
To put our whole selves into praying when we pray
into worshipping when we worship
into singing when we sing.
To put our whole selves into **whatever** it is that **He** calls us to do.

Now, we can be reasonably certain
that the Apostle Paul had never heard of the Hokey Pokey
when he encouraged the Colossians
to put their whole selves into their work for Christ.
But Paul most certainly had the right idea.
He knew from personal experience
what it meant to put his whole self on the line for Jesus Christ!

Reflection:

1. Sing the hymn or read the text together. What specific items does the hymnwriter mention as he exhorts us to give our entire lives to Christ?

2. When you are in worship, are you **fully** present? Or are you physically present but mentally elsewhere? If you are like most people, your attention wanders in worship. How could that be remedied?

3. When you come to choir rehearsal, are you **fully** present? If everyone in the choir were **fully** present for the entire rehearsal, how would things be different?

Prayer:

Lord Jesus
in Your brief time on this earth
there was not a moment when You were not **fully** present.
There was not a moment when You failed
"to put Your whole self in".
Forgive us, Lord,
poor, distracted creatures,
unable to bring ourselves **fully** to anything
always somewhere else in our minds.
Allow us to experience the miracle that You promise
when we "put our whole self in".
Amen!

93

The Shape of Things to Come

Scripture Reading: Romans 9:20–21a and Isaiah 64:8

But who indeed are you, a human being, to argue with God? Will what is molded say to the one who molds it, "Why have you made me like this?" Has the potter no right over the clay . . .

Yet, O Lord, you are our Father; we are the clay and you are our potter; we are all the work of your hand.

Hymn Reference:
Have Thine Own Way, Lord   Adelaide A. Pollard

Meditation:

Is it not you who shape God;
it is God that shapes you.

If then you are the work of God,
await the hand of the Artist
who does all things in due season.

Offer the Potter your heart,
soft and tractable,
and keep the form in which
the artist has fashioned you.

Let your clay be moist,
lest you grow hard and lose
the imprint of the Potter's fingers.
(Iraneus, 2nd century theologian)

Reflection:

1. Have you ever tried to impose your will on another person, to shape someone into what **you** think they **should** be? How did it turn out? Are you willing to share your experience?

2. Being a member of a choir requires that you submit yourself to the leader and allow that person to shape the music you will make. How do you do in this situation?

3. How willing are you to allow God to mold you? How willing are you to fully submit your life to God?

Prayer:

Let us join together and pray in the words of the hymnwriter:

Have thine own way, Lord. Have thine own way!
Thou art the potter; I am the clay.
Mold me and make me after thy will,
while I am waiting, yielding and still.

Have thine own way, Lord! Have thine own way!
Hold o'er my being absolute sway.
Fill with thy Spirit till all shall see
Christ only, always, living in me!
Amen.

Sing a New Song to the Lord

Scripture Reading: Psalm 33:1–3a

Rejoice in the Lord, O you righteous. Praise befits the upright. Praise the Lord with the lyre; make melody to him with the harp of ten strings. Sing to him a new song.

Hymn Reference:
When in Our Music God Is Glorified   Fred Pratt Green

Meditation:

What has happened to all the good, **old** songs?
Why don't we sing them anymore?

My favorite hymn is not in this new hymnal.
Who decided to remove it and why?

s.

ing them.

iip!

ler my feet?
now?
nyway?

96

Reflection:

1. Read the words to the hymn. Sing the hymn. What do you think the writer is saying about music in worship?

2. How does stanza 2 address the issue of new songs, new sounds in worship?

3. Does the Meditation reflect your personal feelings or the feelings of someone you know in your congregation? What would help you or others to feel more comfortable when you "Sing a new song"?

Prayer:

Help us, Lord, to be willing to accept change.
Help us to find something good in what is new and different.
Help us to be willing to grow.
Help us to be willing to be challenged.
Help us to be willing to try new ways of doing things
new ideas
new sounds
new expressions of faith.

Lord, we cherish the hymns of the past.
They are so much a part of us and of our memories.

Enable us to continue to hold them dear
without denying the hymns of the future.
Amen.

Take a Deep Breath

Scripture Reading: Genesis 2:7

*Then the Lord God formed man from the dust of the ground, and breathed
into his nostrils the breath of life; and the man became a living being.*

Hymn Reference:
Breathe on Me, Breath of God   Edwin Hatch

Meditation:

From the moment we take our first breath
we are **alive!**

It is an amazing gift, this thing called **life!**
We have done **nothing** to earn it
and yet when we are born
God breathes life into us
and each one of us becomes a living creature
part of the **human** family.
Life! A miraculous mystery.

* * *

From the moment we confess Christ as Savior
we are **alive** . . . again!

It is an amazing gift, this thing called **new** Life!
We have done **nothing** to earn it
and yet when we are **new**born
the Holy Spirit breathes **new** life into us
and each one of us becomes a **new** creature in Christ
part of **God's** family.
New Life! The most miraculous mystery of all!
Hallelujah!

Reflection:

1. Sing the hymn or read the text together. What does the hymn writer tell us about the power of the Holy Spirit in our lives?

2. In what other forms does the Holy Spirit come to us?

3. Can you think of a time when you felt the presence of the Holy Spirit in the choir? Can you describe the experience?

Prayer:

Spirit of God
sweep over the wilderness of our being
like a mighty wind.
Let each of us take a deep breath
of **New Life.**
Fill us with Your presence
Fill us with Your power.
Fill us with Your peace.
Amen.

Take Me to the Water

Scripture Reading: Genesis 1:1 and Revelation 22:17b

*In the beginning when God created the heavens and the earth, the earth was
a formless void and darkness covered the face of the deep while a wind from
God swept over the face of the waters.*

*And let everyone who is thirsty come. Let anyone who wishes take the water
of life as a gift.*

Hymn Reference:

Take Me to the Water   African-American Spiritual
See Appendix page 141

Meditation:

There's something about water,
something we can't quite put into words
something compelling
something transcendent.

It is the very essence of life itself . . .
a sparkling thematic lifeline
flowing unerringly through the pages of God's word
from the very first verse of Genesis
to the last Chapter of Revelation.
One instance after another.
One story after another.
One miracle after another.
Water!
Water!
And again water!

Water . . . concealing a frightened child in a basket.
Water . . . turning to blood.
Water . . . divided to make a safe path of escape.
Water . . . to baptize the Promised Messiah.
Water . . . suddenly, graciously inexplicably becoming wine.
Water . . . living water offered at the well.
Water in our beginning . . .
a safe place for an unborn child.
Water at our ending . . .
a joyful celebration . . . where else but beside the water?

Reflection:

1. Sing the hymn together. Think about all of the images of water in the Bible. What is your favorite? Can you share it?

2. Can you think of any hymns or popular songs in which water is the central image?

3. What does your own baptism mean to you in the context of your faith?

Prayer:

O God of all the elements
air, earth, sky and sea
in the beginning
when your Spirit hovered over the water
was that sign for us
of how important
how basic
how symbolic
water was to be in our faith journey?

Keep us coming back to the water,
O God
that we may be cleansed
refreshed
and renewed.
Amen.

Telling Stories

Scripture Reading: Matthew 13:34

Jesus told the crowds all these things in parables; without a parable he told them nothing.

Hymn Reference:

I Love to Tell the Story   A. Catherine Hankey

Meditation:

We all seem to love a good story
and the people in Jesus' time were no different.

Jesus used stories to teach the people.
We call them parables . . .
each one a **little** story with a **big** message.

Never mind how long ago these stories were told.
They are always new because they are always true.

We see ourselves in the wayward son
and in the jealous brother who stayed home.
We see ourselves in the Good Samaritan who helped his neighbor
and in the folks who passed by and made excuses.
We see ourselves in the man who built bigger barns
and never got to use them.
We see ourselves in the guests who had no time to come to dinner
and in the fortunate people on the street who got a last-minute invitation.
We see ourselves in the rich man who had no compassion for the poor
and in the poor man who found a place in God's heart.

We have heard the stories
and our lives have been touched and transformed.
Now it is our turn to tell the stories
so that other lives may also be touched and transformed.

Reflection:

1. Sing the hymn or read the text together. Notice that the text writer is not at all reluctant to tell the story, to share the good news. Are you comfortable telling the story of your faith?

2. Which parable is the most meaningful for you personally?

3. How does the ministry of the choir help all of us to share the stories of our faith?

Prayer:

Lord, You told us stories to get our attention.
You told us stories to help us remember the lessons You taught.
You told us stories that showed us how to be
and how **not** to be.
You told us stories to help us change our lives.

And now You ask us to tell Your story to others
by the lives we lead
by the words we speak
by the songs we sing.

Send us forth, Lord
as willing and joyful storytellers
into a world that is hungry to hear the Good News.
Amen.

Temper! Temper!

Scripture Reading: Ephesians 4:26b, 31

Do not let the sun go down on your anger. . . . Put away from you all bitterness and wrath and anger and wrangling and slander, together with all malice, and be kind to one another, tender hearted, forgiving one another, as God in Christ has forgiven you.

Hymn Reference:

Help Us Accept Each Other   Fred Kaan

Meditation:

There is a lot of anger in the world today.
There is a lot of anger in some of us.
We are angry at things that happen in the workplace.
We are angry at some member of our family.
We are angry with our children.
We are angry with ourselves for all our failures
big ones and little ones
for lost opportunities and unfulfilled dreams
for unsuccessful diets and unresolved issues.
We are angry at the violence that has crept into our community.
We are angry at the government for not addressing the things they should.
We are angry at the church for not **being** the church
for selling out its message.
We are angry at the pastor for **not** preaching the truth
or **for** preaching it and making us uncomfortable.
We are angry at choir members who dance in on Sunday morning
and never got to rehearsal this week
or last week.
Most of all we are angry at God for not taking care of all of this.
If God would just do His job, maybe we wouldn't be so angry.

Reflection:

1. Sing the hymn or read the text together. What are some of the strongest statements in the text about anger? What do you think is at the heart of the anger in a person who cannot let go of it?

2. How would you characterize "laughter's healing art"? Can you use laughter to help you deal with the things you are angry about?

3. Is there a situation or a person in the choir that makes you feel angry? Is there any way that you can confront the situation in love? How can your faith help you to deal with your anger?

Prayer:

Lord, you know all about anger.
You threw the money changers out of the temple.
After all
there are some things that we **should** be angry about.

But, Lord, do not allow us to become angry people.
Do not let us go through life
with clenched fists and scowling faces
and harsh words always waiting to be said.

Help us wherever it is Your will
to turn our anger into forgiveness
to turn our anger into compassion
to turn our anger into acceptance.
Amen.

ThanksLiving

Scripture Reading: Psalm 100

*Make a joyful noise to the Lord all the earth. Worship the Lord with glad-
ness; come into his presence with singing. Know that the Lord is God. It is
he that made us and we are his; we are his people and the sheep of his pas-
ture. Enter his gates with thanksgiving and his courts with praise. Give
thanks to him, bless his name. For the Lord is good; his steadfast love
endures forever, and his faithfulness to all generations.*

Hymn Reference:

Let All Things Now Living   Katherine K. Davis

Meditation: A Conversation for Two Readers

Reader 1:   So! How was **your** day?
Reader 2:   Don't ask! (pause) How about yours?
Reader 1:   The same. (pause) Anything new with you?
Reader 2:   My company's been sold. Nobody expected it.
Everybody's job is up for grabs.
Reader 1:   That's tough! It's happening a lot these days!
Reader 2:   Tell me about it! Not much security anywhere!
Reader 1:   That's the truth! Where I work all we hear is downsizing.
You know how **that** goes!
Reader 2:   Yeah! (pause) It's especially hard with the holidays
coming up.
Reader 1:   Boy, you said it! Not much to be thankful for **this** year!
Reader 2:   Nope, I guess not! (pause) Life's a bummer, you know.
Reader 1:   Yeah, it is. (pause) But you know what's really scary?
Reader 2:   What?
Reader 1:   This may be as good as it gets!

Reflection:

1. Do you hear yourself in the meditation? Have you ever had a similar conversation or does the meditation remind you of someone you know?

2. Sing the hymn or read the text together. How does the hymn text reflect the Psalmist's perspective on life?

3. Even in the bleakest times, there is much to be thankful for. Can you think of something or someone for which you are thankful? Can you think of something that happened today or this past week, no matter how insignificant, for which you are thankful?

Prayer: A Litany of Thanksgiving for Choir and Solo Reader

Gracious God
we give you thanks for all You have done for us
for the gift of life
for the gift of this earth and its beauty
for work and for health.

Now thank we all our God with hearts and hands and voices

We give thanks for all those who have touched our lives
for family and friends
for teachers and mentors
for all those who have helped to make our lives better in any way.

Now thank we all our God with hearts and hands and voices

We give thanks for this church and its leaders and teachers
for this community of believers
for fellowship, for friendship and for faith
for sacrament, for sacrifice and for song.

Now thank we all our God with hearts and hands and voices

In all the conditions of this life, O God,
help us to remember to be thankful.
Amen.

Through Thick and Thin

Scripture Reading: Romans 8:37–39

> *. . . in all these things we are more than conquerors through him who loved us. For I am convinced that neither death, nor life, nor angels, nor rulers, nor things present, nor things to come, nor powers, nor height nor depth, nor anything else in all creation will be able to separate us from the love of God in Christ Jesus our Lord.*

Hymn Reference:

Jesus Calls Us O'er the Tumult   Cecil Alexander

Meditation:

We meet God in the extremities of life.

In Beginnings and Endings . . .
children born, parents dying
friendships begun, marriages ended
morning coffee and midnight reverie
He is with us!

In Joys and Sorrows . . .
homecomings and partings
healings and hurts
meals and miseries . . .
He is with us!

In the New and in the Old . . .
new resolutions, old habits
new homes, old heartaches
new loves, old angers
He is with us!

In the Beautiful and in the Blemished . . .
the blaze of fall, the blight of famine
the quick young mind, the twisted disfigured spine
the soaring eagle, the oil-drenched egret
He is with us!

He calls to us
in our joys and in our sorrows
in our times of plenty and in our times of need
in the best and in the worst of our days.

Are we listening?

Reflection:

1. Sing the hymn or read the text together. What imagery does the hymnwriter use in the first stanza to describe life?

2. Can you think of a time of great joy or great sorrow when God seemed especially near?

3. There are joys and sorrows in music ministry both for the leaders and for the choir. Can you think of a time of great joy or great sorrow in this choir when God's presence could not be denied?

Prayer:

There is no denying it, Lord.
We know You are with us
in all our comings and goings
but somehow
we are most aware of Your presence
when we rejoice
and when we weep.

We meet you, Lord, in the extremities of life
beside the cradle
and at the cross.
Amen.

The Weary Saints

Scripture Reading: Luke 4:8

Jesus answered him, It is written, "Worship the Lord your God, and serve only him."

Hymn Reference:
Rejoice in God's Saints Fred Pratt Green

Meditation:

Sometimes I think about the saints
those champions of the gospel.
They seem somehow superhuman
superpowered
superblessed
bigger than life
and they make **me** feel inadequate.
I have to remind myself that they struggled too
that they doubted too
that they were human just as I am.

I try to imagine David
after a long, difficult day
his shoulders slumped
his brow furrowed
his youth slipping away.

I catch a glimpse of Jacob
limping and sore
after an all-night wrestling match with God.
His hip is bruised and throbbing.
He winces with every step.

I hear Mary sighing
tired of worrying about her son
tired of his prolonged absences
and his strange ways.
"Why couldn't he have been just an ordinary boy?"

I hear Paul calling out in the night
see him tossing in his sleep
obsessed with his mission
unable to rest even when he might.

It is good to hear the stories of the accomplishments of the saints
and of their strengths
but in some strange way
it is the vision of their weariness
of their humanity
that renews me for my own journey of faith.

Reflection:

1. Sing the hymn or read the text together. When you think of God's saints, what is the first name that comes to mind?

2. When you need to be renewed, whose story in the Bible is the one you hold on to? Why?

3. Is there anyone you know personally or have known who you might categorize as "a saint"? Can you share the reason you feel as you do about that person?

Prayer:

O God of the saints
both triumphant and weary
help us to see their struggles as well as their victories.
Help us to see that it wasn't all great deeds and miracles for them.
It was sweat and tears and calluses and heartache.
It was sleepless nights and dreary, dog-tired days.
It was moments of doubt and fear and bewilderment and frustration.

Thank you, O God, for the reminder of what we share.
Amen.

Welcome to the Middle Ages!

Scripture Reading: I Corinthians 3:11

For no one can lay any foundation other than the one that has been laid; that foundation is Jesus Christ.

Hymn Reference:

How Firm a Foundation   J. Rippon

Meditation:

Can you remember your first gray hair?
If any image can threaten your foundation
this one can.

Maybe you were going through a troubled time
when it happened
or maybe it was just an ordinary day
ordinary that is until you noticed that one significant sign
that time was no longer your friend.

It may have been a symbolic occasion for you
when you found yourself entering
the unexplored and frightening wilderness of Middle Age
and looking back
you saw the Red Sea of Youth close behind you.
There was no way to go but forward
into the desert of eventual senility.

Like the Hebrews
you probably looked back longingly at what you were leaving behind.
Like the Hebrews
you probably grumbled over what certainly lay ahead.
And like the Hebrews
you probably had serious doubts about God's ability
to take you safely into the future.

Did you find the "firm foundation" of youth crumbling around you?
Did you wonder if your faith was equal to this
unsettling and unexpected crisis?
If you were like most of us, you entered middle age at best with reluctance
and at worst kicking and screaming all the way!

112

Reflection:

1. Sing the hymn or read the text together. What words of comfort does the hymnwriter offer for a Middle Age crisis?

2. Can you remember when you were the youngest singer in the choir and everyone else seemed so old? How do you feel now?

3. What affect does aging have on your music ministry? on your voice? on your stamina? on your enthusiasm? on your willingness to try new musical styles?

Prayer:

You understand aging, Lord.
You are older than creation
and yet You come to us each year newborn.

Calm our anxious fears.
Help us to renew the firm foundation of our faith in You.
Help us to let go of our youth gracefully
and to submit ourselves and our fears to You
knowing that You hold the future in Your loving hands.
Amen.

Welcoming the Stranger

Scripture Reading: Genesis 18:1–8

The Lord appeared to Abraham by the oaks of Mamre as he sat at the entrance of his tent in the heat of the day. He looked up and saw three men standing hear him. When he saw them, he ran from the tent entrance to meet them and bowed down to the ground. He said, "My lord, if I find favor with you, do not pass by your servant. Let a little water be brought, and wash your feet, and rest yourselves under the tree. Let me bring a little bread, that you may refresh yourselves, and after that you may pass on . . ."

And Abraham hastened into the tent to Sarah, and said, "Make ready quickly three measures of choice flour, knead it, and make cakes." Abraham ran to the herd, and took a calf, tender and good, and gave it to the servant, who hastened to prepare it. Then he took curds of milk and the calf that he had prepared and set before them; and he stood by them under the tree while they ate.

Hymn Reference:

Christians We Have Met to Worship   George Adkins
alt. Bryan Jeffrey Leech

Meditation:

I saw a stranger yestereen:
I put food in the eating place,
drink in the drinking place,
music in the listening place;
and in the blessed name of the Triune
he blessed myself and my house,
my cattle and my dear ones,
and the lark said her song
often, often, often,
goes the Christ in the stranger's guise
often, often, often,
goes the Christ in the stranger's guise
Old Gaelic Rune

Reflection:

1. Read or sing the hymn together. The hymnwriter tells us that Christ welcomes us. How can we make others feel welcome in our church? In our choir?

2. Can you think of a time in your life when you were a stranger and someone did not welcome you? What did they do or not do that made you feel unwelcome?

3. How could our congregation and this choir do a better job of welcoming the stranger?

Prayer:

Forgive me, O God,
when I do not do my part
to make the stranger feel welcome.

Forgive me
when I do not offer a smile
when I do not offer my hand
when I do not offer coffee or a hot drink
when I do not offer a place of refuge
when I do not offer comfort.

Forgive me, O God,
when I do not welcome the new member to the choir.
Forgive me
when I forget how it feels to be a stranger.
Forgive me
when I forget how it feels to be an outsider.

Remind me
that it is You, O God
who visits us again and again
as a stranger in our midst.
Amen.

What Happens in the Silence?

Scripture Reading: Habakkuk 2:20

But the Lord is in his holy temple: let all the earth keep silence before him!

Hymn Reference:
Let All Mortal Flesh Keep Silence **tr.** Gerard Moultrie
From Liturgy of St. James, 4th c.

Meditation:

Those of us who make music
know that the silences are as important as the notes.
The listener knows it too.

The silence **before** the song
is ripe with expectation.
The silence **after** the song
is rich with the resonance of that final chord
and with the lingering essence of the message.
The silences **within** the song
provide balance
drama
space
and often a surprise or two.

Music cannot be all sound.
There must be silent spaces within it.

Life is the same.
There must be silent spaces.
And it is in those silent spaces
that we are most likely to meet God.

Advent is a time of joyous expectation.
Sometimes there are no words to express our yearning.
Sometimes we just have to be silent and wait.

Reflection:

1. Sing the first stanza of the hymn. How does the music reflect the text?

2. Do you allow for silent space in your own life? If so, how does that silence affect you? What might you do to provide more silent spaces in your life?

3. Can you think of a time in rehearsal or in worship or in a particular anthem when silence had a profound effect on you, a time when you felt undeniably aware of God's presence?

Prayer:

O God of Silence and Sound
help us to seek out the silent spaces in our lives
where You can meet us.

In this season of Advent
we are holding our breath
unable to speak
listening with our hearts
anxious for the first sign of Your coming
anxious for a sound of a baby's cry.

Hear our silent prayer of welcome!

(Allow a few moments for a silent prayer, then continue.)

Come, O come, Emmanuel!
Amen

What's Love Got to Do with It?

Scripture Reading: John 15:12–13

This is my commandment, that you love one another as I have loved you. No one has greater love that this, to lay down one's life for one's friends.

Hymn Reference:
What Wondrous Love Is This?   American Folk Hymn

Meditation:

Is there anything you would be willing to die for?
A person?
A cause?

Is there anything that matters more to you than your own life?
A person?
A cause?

Is there anyone you know who would be willing to give up their life for you?

Such a love is not easy to understand.
Such a love is not easy to find.
Chances are if **you** love someone that much
it's not because of **what** they have done
it's because of **who** they are.
Chances are if someone loves **you** that much
it's not because of **what** you have done
it's because of **who** you are.

We cannot fully grasp the idea of sacrificial love
but when we are faced with the question
our hearts seem to instinctively know the answer.

Reflection:

1. Sing the hymn or read the text together. The hymnwriter refers to sacrificial love as "wondrous love". Can you think of any other adjectives to describe it?

2. Have you ever known anyone who sacrificed their life for someone else? Can you tell their story?

3. In your opinion, what hymn or anthem best captures the theme of sacrificial love?

Prayer:

Lamb of God
you showed us by example what sacrificial love is all about.
You showed us what it meant to give your life away.
You showed us what it meant to be a servant.

Work in our hearts, Lord,
that we may learn to fully love You
that we may learn to offer ourselves as a living sacrifice to You
that we may learn to love others more than we love ourselves.
Amen.

What's That in Your Hand?

Scripture Reading: Exodus 4:2–3a

The Lord said to him, "What is that in your hand?" He said, "A staff." And he said, "Throw it on the ground."

Hymn Reference:

Take My Life   Frances R. Havergal

Meditation:

Christianity has two central themes:
letting go and grabbing hold.

We have to let go of our old life
to grab hold of new life.

We have to let go of our sins
to grab hold of forgiveness.

We have to let go of darkness
to grab hold of the light.

We have to let go of the world
to grab hold of the Kingdom of God.

We have to let go of the past
to grab hold of the future.

We have to let go of our own agenda
to grab hold of God's agenda.

If our hands are busy holding on to the wrong things
we can't reach out for the right ones.

Is God asking you to let go of something today
so that you can grab hold of something better?
A job?
A person?
A habit?
A plan you hold for your future?

What's that in your hand?
Can you let it go?

Reflection:

1. Sing the hymn or read the text together. What are the specific things that the hymnwriter let go of?

2. The third verse of the hymn talks about the voice, laying it down, giving it over to God for God to use as He will. If you were to completely dedicate your voice to God, how would that change your life? How would it change your commitment to the choir? How would it change your conversation?

3. Can you think of specific individuals in the Bible who let go of something to grab hold of God's plan for their lives?

Prayer:

O God of the Ultimate Challenge
give us the courage to let go
of whatever holds us back
of whatever we love better than You
of whatever **we** have planned for the future
in order to grab hold of what **you** have planned for **us**
for the furthering of your kingdom.
Amen.

When in Doubt, Look Up!

Scripture Reading: Matthew 17:20b–21

*For truly I tell you, if you have faith the size of a mustard seed, you will say
to this mountain, "Move from here to there,"' and it will move; and nothing
will be impossible for you.*

Hymn Reference:
My Faith Looks Up to Thee   Ray Palmer

Meditation:

Let's talk a little bit about faith.
Why is it that we have so little?
Why is that what we have is so misdirected?

How can we so easily trust in temporal things
when eternal things go begging?

If faith has such power
why do we feel so powerless?

If faith can move mountains
why can't we at least stir up a little dust?

The truth is
our faith seems to be looking everywhere
but up.

Maybe that's the problem!

Reflection:

1. Read the hymn text aloud. Why is looking up important to the believer? You may want to make this hymn a part of your daily devotional time this week.

2. **What** or **who** keeps you from having a strong faith?

3. What hymn or song is most helpful to you when your faith is weak? Why?

Prayer:

Forgive us, Lord, for faith without wings.

Forgive us for faith that hugs the shore
when it could walk on the water.

Forgive us for faith that would send the crowd away hungry
when they could have been fed.

Forgive us for our unbelief, Lord.
We are like Abraham and Sarah . . .
giggling when we should be giving thanks . . .
shopping for a wheelchair instead of a baby buggy.

Remind us that You **can** do the impossible, Lord.
Help us to **expect** the impossible.

Most of all, Lord, remind us to look up!

Amen.

Whole Notes, Etc.

Scripture Reading: Mark 10:52

Jesus said to him, "Go; your faith has made you whole."

Hymn Reference:
Lord Jesus, I Long to Be Perfectly Whole   James L. Nicholson

Meditation:

What is a rehearsal all about?
Are we here to learn the fundamentals?
And if so exactly **which** fundamentals are we talking about?

We talk a lot about the value of each note . . .
but how often do we mention the value of each person?

We worry about giving whole notes their full due
but not about whether we ourselves are whole.

We talk about observing the rests, the silences . . .
but not about how we yearn for silence in our hectic days.

We try to make sense of the words we sing . . .
but we can't make sense of our lives.

We try to sing in harmony with one another . . .
when our families are full of discord.

We sing about peace and love and joy . . .
and wish we could grab hold of them.

We sing about prayer . . .
and wish we really knew how.

We sing about God
and wish we knew **Him** . . . really knew Him.

What is missing in our time together?
What fundamentals do we need to be sure to address?

124

Reflection:

1. Sing the hymn or read the first stanza of the hymn together. What do you think the hymnwriter means by "perfectly whole"? What does that phrase mean to you?

2. The demands of rehearsal mean that the particulars of music must be attended to. But each person who sings brings special needs. What special need do you have that you can share?

3. What would it take for this choir to become more spiritually nurturing? How can this be accomplished within the confines of the allotted time?

Prayer:

O God of Song and of the Singer
We thank You for our special talents.

We thank You that those talents bring us together here in this place.
We make an offering to You of the gifts You have bestowed upon us
and we pray Your blessing on our offering of song.

As we minister to others through music
we confess that we ourselves are needy.
You alone know those needs.
You alone can fill the empty places in our lives.
You alone can make us whole.
We offer You our song and ourselves
for the good of Your kingdom.
Amen.

Who Would Send a Baby?

Scripture Reading: John 3:16–17

*For God so loved the world that he gave his only Son, so that everyone who
believes in him may not perish but may have eternal life. Indeed, God did
not send the Son into the world to condemn the world but in order that the
world might be saved through him.*

Hymn Reference:

God's Love Made Visible   Dave Brubeck

Meditation:

The people knew the promises.
They knew a Messiah would come.
They knew He would offer a new and better alternative.
They knew the world would be different after his coming.
They waited
and they waited
and they waited.
And when at last the time had come
and the promise was to be fulfilled
even after all that waiting
they were not prepared
because God didn't do what they expected . . .
God surprised them.
Yes, God did indeed surprise them . . . with a baby!
Who would send a baby?
Only God!

Reflection:

1. Read the text of Dave and Iola Brubeck's unusual and captivating hymn, "God's Love Made Visible!" How does this hymn, in both text and music, help to capture some of God's surprising and unexpected spirit?

2. If you had been in God's place, who would you have sent to fulfill the promises?

3. Has God ever surprised you through an anthem or a hymn or something that happened in the choir?

Prayer:

O God of surprises
O God of the unexpected

You have blessed us with the ultimate surprise.
You have graced us with the ultimate unexpected gift.

You have placed that unexpected gift
in a surprising place
where we would never expect to find it.
And you have brought a surprising and eccentric group together
in that place to be the first to discover the gift
shepherds . . . kings . . . sheep . . . cattle.

Enable us to come to know You better
through Your surprising and unexpected acts.
Amen.

Worrying Our Way to Christmas

Scripture Reading: Isaiah 40:1

"Comfort, O comfort my people," says your God.

Hymn Reference:
Comfort, Comfort You My People   Johannes G. Olearius
tr. Catherine Winkworth 1863

Meditation:

Every year at Christmas we hear the story anew.
And somehow it comes out as it should.
But I'm a classic worry wart.
Every year I worry as the big day approaches.
What if something goes wrong **this** time?
What if something terrible happens to ruin the story?

I worry about Mary and Joseph.
What if they don't make it to Bethlehem in time?
What if they can't wake the innkeeper?
What if there is someone already staying in the stable?

What if the shepherds don't get the message?
What if they can't find the place?
What if nobody will stay with the sheep?

What if the angels don't show up?
What if the kings take a wrong turn?
What if the baby turns out to be a girl?

What if I sleep through the whole thing?

Reflection:

1. Read the text of the hymn. The comfort Isaiah speaks about is comfort in time of oppression, comfort in time of warfare, comfort in time of misery. But in this day and age many of us need comfort from our fretful approach to life, comfort from all the things that worry us. We need God's peace as much as the people of Isaiah's time. What are the things you are worried about in this Advent season?

2. Some of us are chronic worriers. The meditation gives us a picture of one who worries even when they know how things will turn out. Do you worry needlessly?

3. How can your ministry in the choir help you to lay aside your worries this Christmas season?

Prayer:

Won't you help us, Lord,
to stop our worrying?

In this season of Advent
help us to await Your coming
with a sense of joy
and with the comfort of Your peace in our hearts.

Instead of hurrying
scurrying
and worrying our way to Christmas
help us to focus on the bright blazing star
that announces hope and healing for all the world.
Amen.

You Are There!

Scripture Reading: Matthew 26:36a

Then Jesus went with them to a place called Gethsemane.

Hymn Reference:
Go to Dark Gethsemane   James Montgomery

Meditation:

It is midnight.
You are alone in the Garden of Gethsemane.
You see Jesus off in the distance with the disciples.
They are moving toward you.
You hear Him speak to them briefly.
Then He moves away from them deeper into the garden
near to where you are standing
He doesn't see You.
He kneels there, head down
and for a time the only sound you hear is His breathing.

There are no stars tonight and only a sliver of moon.
The Garden is still and the air seems heavy and dense.
Jesus is close enough to touch.

At last You can hear Him begin to pray aloud.
He pauses often, choosing His words with care.
His voice becomes more insistent, pleading
and you can see that even on this cool night
He is perspiring heavily.

Suddenly there is silence, then a great sigh.
Something seems to be resolved in his mind.
Jesus rises and moves away, toward the disciples.
He stands looking down at them
and somehow He seems more alone than ever.
They have fallen asleep.

Reflection:

1. Sing the first stanza of the hymn or read the first stanza of the text together. What do you think the textwriter wants you to see when you "Go to Dark Gethsemane"?

2. Have you ever had to face anything difficult all alone? How did you feel? How would it have been different if someone had been with you?

3. What do you think the Choir's responsibility should be during Lent? What would make the season and its message more personal for you?

Prayer:

Lord Jesus
let me travel this Lenten journey with You.
Let me kneel beside You in the Garden.
Let me stand with You before Pilate
and help You carry the cross to Calvary.
Let me hear You cry out in those last moments
and let me weep with those who gather at the foot of the cross.

Make it a new story for me, Lord, this year
so that I can sing it
and tell it
and live it
with a real sense of Your suffering
Your sacrifice
and Your pain.
Amen.

Practical Ideas for Choir Singers Who Want a Richer Spiritual Life

Be a more faithful choir member. Your faithfulness (or lack of it) affects other singers. Be a positive influence by your attendance.

Try to avoid a negative attitude
    in your family life
    at work
    in the choir
Be honest but avoid being critical.

Write a supportive letter to someone in the choir or in the church who may need a lift.

Do a kind deed for someone in the choir or for one of the church staff. Whatever you do, do it in secret.

Guard the reputation of others in the choir and in your church.

Take a stand in your church if some issue of social injustice arises.

Support the choir, your director and your pastor(s) with your prayers.

Make a commitment to spend time in prayer daily . . . and keep that commitment.

Be willing and open to the needs of other choir members. Make it possible for them to express their joys, concerns and prayer requests.

Think of your membership in the choir as a ministry and approach everything you do in rehearsal and in worship in that spirit. Always offer your best effort.

When you are in rehearsal or in worship learn to focus fully on what you are doing at that very moment. Do not allow yourself to be distracted by outside influences or the day's difficulties. Concentrate on the message of the anthems and the hymns you sing and allow the making of music to be a devotional experience for you.

Let go of busyness and unnecessary rushing in your life. Ask for God's help to enable you to find a sense of calm in your daily living.

Ask God's help to make a positive change in your life.

Keep a journal of your spiritual progress . . . your concerns, your prayers, your struggles, your victories.

Fast from television for a week. Note the effect on your life and on the life of your family.

Take one day when you concentrate on thanking God for all He has created.

Let the Bible be a regular influence in your life. Choose a method of daily reading which suits your life style and stick with it. Let God reveal Himself to you through His word.

The Ten Commandments for Church Choirs

I. Thou shalt keep the joy of thy calling ever before thee;
it shall protect thee from despair
and shall cover thee when the day doth vex thee sorely.

II. Thou shalt remember that thou art chosen
to lead the people's worship in song
and not to seek vain and foolish flattery.
Yea, thou shalt put all manner of worldly thoughts behind thee on the Sabbath
lest they draw the hearts and minds of the people toward thee
and away from the worship of the one true God.

III. Thou shalt come before the congregation with a joyful spirit
and with a song in thy heart;
though they may try thy patience with their lack of understanding
and withhold from thee words of favor.

IV. Thou shalt honor thy director
and lift him/her up with prayers and deeds of kindness.
Thou shalt come before him/her with a compliant and willing spirit
lest he/she lose heart and falter.

V. Remember the Sabbath to keep it holy.
Thou shalt honor the Lord on that day with thy best gifts.
Thou shalt not dishonor thy calling
with late rising
or with wicked and perverse weekend travel.

VI. Thou shalt not covet thy neighbor's robe
nor his hymnbook
nor her choir folder
nor his pencil
nor anything that is thy neighbor's.

VII. Thou shalt honor the hymns and liturgies of the people
and render them with diligence and care.
Thou shalt not forsake thy heritage in song.
Neither shalt thou bring a stubborn spirit
to war against that which is new and unsettling.

VIII. Thou shalt not forsake the ways of the righteous
but shall come before the Lord with clean hands and a pure heart
rejoicing always in the knowledge of the Lord
and offering up prayers and praise and thanksgiving unto Him.

IX. Thou shalt love thy singing neighbor as thyself
upholding her in prayer
joining him in fellowship
and honoring and caring for each one
as a brother or sister in Christ.

X. Thou shalt bring joy . . .
the joy of thy calling
and the joy of thy salvation . . .
to the hearts of all about thee;
to thy spouse and thy children
to thy friends and to thy family
and to all whom thou mayest meet upon thy way.

Bibliography
(Selected Materials in the area of Spiritual Formation)

Anderson, Andy. 1978. *Fasting Changed My Life.* Nashville, TN: Broadman Press.

Beltz, Bob. 1996. *Becoming a Man of Prayer (A Seven-Week Strategy Based on the Instructions of Jesus).* Colorado Springs, CO: NavPress.

Brussat, Frederic and Mary Ann es. 1996. *Spiritual Literacy (Reading the Sacred in Everyday Life).* New York: Scribner.

Bundesen, Lynn. 1995. *One Prayer at a Time (A Day-to-Day Path to Spiritual Growth).* New York: Simon & Schuster.

Carter, Jimmy. 1996. *Living Faith.* New York: Random House.

Fischer, John. 1995. *Be Thou My Vision. (Daily Inspiriation from the Greatest Hymns of All Time).* Ann Arbor, MI: Vine Books.

Foster, Richard J. Revised Edition 1998. *Celebration of Discipline (The Path to Spiritual Growth).* San Francisco: Harper/San Francisco.

Greeley, Andrew M. 1995. *Windows (A Prayer Journal).* New York: Crossroad.

Harris, Maria. 1991 *Dance of the Spirit (The Seven Steps of Women's Spirituality).* New York: Bantam Books.

Housdan, Roger. 1995. *Retreat (Time Apart for Silence and Solitude).* New York: Harper/San Francisco.

Hybels, Bill. 1988. *Too Busy Not to Pray (Slowing Down to Be with God)* Downers Grove, IL: InterVarsity Press.

Jones, Laurie Beth. 1997. *Jesus in Blue Jeans (A Practical Guide to Everyday Spirituality).* New York: Hyperion.

Klug, Ronald. 1993. *How to Keep a Spiritual Journal.* Minneapolis: Augsburg.

Link, Mark, S. J. 1990. *Prayer Paths (Search for Serenity in an Age of Stress).* Allen, TX: Tabor Publishing.

Morgan, Henry, Ed. 1991. *Approaches to Prayer (Resource Book for Groups and Individuals).* Bristol, UK: Longdunn Press, Ltd.

Moore, Thomas. 1992. *Care of the Soul (A Guide for Cultivating Depth and Sacredness in Everyday Life).* New York: Harper Collins.

Norris, Kathleen. 1996. *The Cloister Walk.* New York: Riverhead Books.

Peck, M. Scott, M.D. 1993. *Farther Along the Road Less Traveled (The Unending Journey Toward Spiritual Growth).* New York: Simon & Schuster.

Smith, James Bryan. 1993. *A Spiritual Formation Workbook (Small Group Resources for Nurturing Christian Growth).* San Francisco: Harper/San Francisco.

Tirabassi, Becky. 1994. *Wild Things Happen When I Pray (Praying People into the Kingdom).* Grand Rapids, MI: Zondervan Publishing House.

Twerski, Abraham J., M.D. 1991. *I'd Like to Call for Help, But I Don't Know the Number (The Search for Spirituality in Everyday Life).* New York: Henry Holtke and Company.

Wold, Wayne L. 1997. *Tune My Heart to Sing (Devotions for Choirs Based on the Revised Common Lectionary).* Minneapolis, MN: Augsburg Fortress.

Appendix

Peace Like a River

Traditional   Traditional

1. I've got peace like a riv-er, I've got peace like a
2. I've got love like an o-cean, I've got love like an
3. I've got joy like a foun-tain, I've got joy like a

riv-er, I've got peace like a riv-er in my soul, I've got
o-cean, I've got love like an o-cean in my soul, I've got
foun-tain, I've got joy like a foun-tain in my soul, I've got

peace like a riv-er, I've got peace like a riv-er,
love like an o-cean, I've got love like an o-cean,
joy like a foun-tain, I've got joy like a foun-tain,

I've got peace like a riv-er in my soul. (my soul)
I've got love like an o-cean in my soul. (my soul)
I've got joy like a foun-tain in my soul. (my soul)

INTROIT: The Lord Is in His Holy Temple

For Unison Choir

MARY KAY BEALL

JOHN CARTER

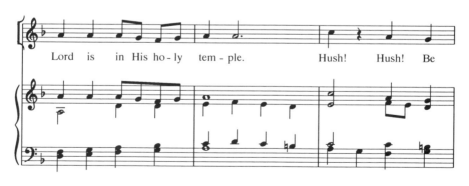

still. The Lord is in His tem-ple now, let all cre-a-tion hum-bly bow. _____ Let all be si-lent be-fore Him now. Hush! Hush! Hush! Hush! Hush! Hush! Be still. _____ Be still.

decresc. *slowing* mp opt. div.

Christ Has No Hands but Your Hands

MARY KAY BEALL   JOHN CARTER

1. Christ has no hands but your hands to heal the world's in-firm-i-ties, to touch the hurt-ing, com-fort, calm, to of-fer heal-ing balm.
2. Christ has no feet but your feet to walk the paths of right-eous-ness, to seek the sad, to lead the lost, and nev-er count the cost.
3. Christ has no arms but your arms to lift the fall-en, hold the faint, to bear the heav-y weight of grief for all who seek re-lief.
4. Christ has no heart but your heart to love the lone-ly, prize the weak, to cry for ev-ery trou-bled soul, to make the wound-ed whole.
5. Christ has no voice but your voice to sing the songs of joy and peace, to shout the news of vic-to-ry that sets the cap-tive free.

Take Me to the Water

For SATB Voices, Unaccompanied

Traditional Spiritual

Arr. JAY EDWARDS

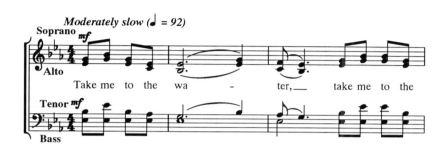

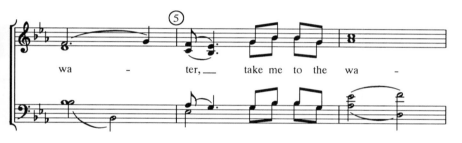

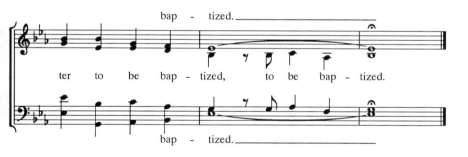

141